Journeys

Stefan Zweig

Translated by Will Stone

Modern Voices

Modern Voices
Published by Hesperus Press Limited
4 Rickett Street, London SW6 1RU
www.hesperuspress.com

First published in 1902–40
First published by Hesperus Press Limited, 2010

Essays taken from *Auf Riesen* © Williams Verlag, Zurich, 1976
Introduction, English language translation and photographs © Will Stone, 2010

Designed and typeset by Fraser Muggeridge studio
Printed in Jordan by Jordan National Press

ISBN: 978-1-84391-458-7

Contents

Introduction

A day of travel just like so many others over these last years. Is it because the world shakes on its foundations that one is so used to living in perpetual movement? Is it the premonition that a time is approaching when countries will erect barriers between them, so you yearn to breathe quickly, while you still can, a little of the world's air? Whatever it might be, to travel is for me no longer something foreign, but almost natural. One breaks free with more force from one's ties and habits, of one's home and possessions – both become insecure, they no longer miss you. Two suitcases, one containing my clothes, the material necessities, the other my manuscripts, the reserve for work and spirit, and so one is everywhere at home. And if the meaning of life consists in relentlessly discovering in the temporal and intellectual new forms of freedom, it is better perhaps to live with the least possible constraints, the art of leaving behind oneself, without sentimentality, a good portion of one's past.

Journal entry, 27th September 1935,
journey from Paris to London

To merely ascribe to the celebrated Austrian writer Stefan Zweig the title 'inveterate traveller' – as one of those who may find literary inspiration, temporary existential relief and inner fulfilment of a kind in the act and the art of travel – to lump him in with other prolific writer-travellers, would be to fail properly to understand the absolutely primary importance of travel or the 'journey' to his particular existence. For Zweig, travel, and European travel especially, was unquestionably the fulcrum of his entire adult life. When Zweig talks of travel he means travel by train, taking advantage of a complex rail network that found its golden age in the first half of the twentieth century, allowing the refined, erudite traveller to indulge in the comforting illusion of domestic privacy in the small furnished compartment, wood-lined carriages studded with pictures, the handsome dining car, the attentive steward… giving the impression one was somehow still at home but also on the move.

In the journal entry above, Zweig himself articulates the extent to which, by 1935, travel had become not a departure from home, but a home in itself. By this time, Zweig was no longer travelling with a light heart for cultural enrichment alone, to escape a sterile patch in his domestic life or to enhance literary relationships, to perform readings or attend lectures, to write a commission on a certain place for a leading German news-paper, to tease out of a fellow writer another manuscript or letter for his voluminous collection, or any other reason that made up the objectives for the countless journeys that span his working lifetime. In 1934, Zweig – a Jew and committed pacifist, whose celebrated novellas, novels and popular biographies were to burn on pyres in university courtyards across Germany – had abruptly terminated a period of fifteen years living in Salzburg and was if not yet running at full tilt, then jogging purposefully from snowballing Nazi tyranny. Seeking sanctuary in England, Zweig settled first in London then later in Bath, a town enclosed by a rural landscape that reminded the exile of his beloved Salzburg. Then, as Britain was in turn drawn into the war, came the affront of the Austrian-born author being labelled an 'enemy alien': he a Jew and victim of the Nazi state! Somewhat unhelp-fully indecisive in his personal life, yet prone to dramatic de-cisiveness when events constituted a direct attack on his person, Zweig embarked for the USA along with his new wife, formerly his secretary, Lotte Altmann. Soon afterwards he moved on to Brazil, a country that had previously seduced him, where he was to remain until the combination of an insidious depression about the internecine events in Europe and the unexpected loneliness of his exile's vigil culminated in his suicide, alongside his wife, in their small house in Petropolis in February 1942. In the above journal entry, made en route from Paris to London, we have an insight into Zweig's thoughts as he sensed a perhaps permanent life on the road courtesy of Hitler, an imminent jettisoning of an old life, now outlawed, for a new unknown one, in which a man with two suitcases and a passport would attempt to breathe what was left of 'the world's air' before the hatch of war came down again. These first feelers of anxiety signal the lighting of the fuse that burned on ever more powerfully to reach, seven years later, the explosive ending none had foreseen.

Zweig's first precocious literary achievements when barely out of his teens were confined to the self-regarding circles of turn-of-the-century literary Vienna. Destined by way of birth and social position to prosper within a privileged artistic milieu where, at least for him, success came too easily, the youthful Zweig sensed that if he was to understand properly what it meant to be human he would have to extricate himself from that rarefied nepotistic circus and get his fingernails dirty in the soil of a wider Europe and beyond. First stop was Berlin, where he attempted rather unconvincingly to live for a time the life of a bohemian. This otherwise undistinguished period of 'slumming it' in the more exotic and edgy dens of artistic Berlin was however crucial in terms of contacts, namely his meeting with the influential political figure Walter Rathenau, who impressed on Zweig in no uncertain terms the need for him radically to expand his horizons by travel. Next stop was Belgium, symbolically the crossroads of Europe, where Zweig wrote a postcard in shaky French from Bruges requesting a meeting in Brussels with the famous poet Emile Verhaeren. Thus began a deep friendship of mutual respect that fostered important literary accomplishments on both sides, interrupted only by the outbreak of war in 1914 and Verhaeren's tragic death two years later, when he was crushed by a train in Rouen station. Verhaeren's presence in both poetic and personal terms overwhelmed the cosseted Zweig. The fervent Whitmanesque visions of Verhaeren's poetry and his ever passionate, ever curious, always fair and humane nature, the sheer human impact of this resolutely European-minded man was no less than a revelation to Zweig, heralding a new way of thinking and living that shaped the remainder of his life. Ever faithful to Verhaeren, whom he saw, before the First World War tore into such lofty ideals, as one of the key European thinkers, those who together could usher in a vanguard of like-minded spirits to secure a united Europe, Zweig not only wrote an important biography of the Belgian poet, translated into several languages (including English), but secured his reputation in Germany by translating his poetry. Hence we find in the body of Zweig's work a slightly disproportionate number of essays relating to Belgian locations. At Verhaeren's urging, which no doubt also influenced a young Rilke to make the same journey shortly after, Zweig sought out the Flemish towns of Bruges, Ghent and Antwerp, while during this same period he also travelled south to Provence, to discover Arles, Avignon, Tarascon, St Rémy and Les Baux. Here Zweig encountered the Provençal landscape of a century ago, still enjoying a late flowering of its unique customs, following the renewed exposure and safeguarding of its traditions by its indefatigable native son, the poet Frédéric Mistral.

Thus we have a crop of essays from the period 1902 to 1906, starting with 'The Season in Ostend', in which we are given a glimpse of the almost unimaginable luxuries and largely upper-crust decadence of northern Europe's leading coastal resort, as the town transformed into a glittering playground for the smart set's summer season and reverted to a lowly fishing port during the dead period of autumn and winter. It is pertinent to read this account and observe the rather drably materialist though in another sense eerily nostalgic Ostend of today, utterly unrecognisable from the grandiose portrait Zweig painted a century before. Ostend never recovered its former grandeur after being levelled by bombs during the Second World War, and ever since has been condemned to pick resignedly at its own architectural scab, the town's authorities convulsively rebuilding, levelling what remains of its more meaningful past, gentrifying its old venerable art museum into a sterile complex of fashion boutiques, for example, and leaving behind the famously immense curve of the old sea front a monstrous showpiece for bleak functionality at the expense of aesthetic enrichment.

Also included in this period is the curious essay on Hyde Park, where Zweig attempts to articulate the unique character of the largest of London's parks, to sift from the misty English heath a psychology of place. Here one sees to the fore, perhaps for the first time, the gently probing but determined method of Zweig, where a repetitive handling of the impressionistic material finally distils the nuances he is looking for. Zweig portrays Edwardian-era Hyde Park as a miraculously situated giant garden for the robust English to reveal their leisure and sporting proclivities, whilst at the same time retaining an air of peace and otherness from the metropolis that heaves in on all sides. The result is unexpectedly intriguing.

It would probably be true to say that as Zweig gains experience as both a traveller and a writer, especially after the trauma of world war, his essays exhibit more depth and his concerns take on more urgency. 'Antwerp' (1914), 'Requiem for a hotel' (1918) and 'Ypres' (1928) reflect this trend. In the first we learn of the obsession of Napoleon with that vital port town. Zweig's evident satisfaction, his determination to acknowledge the schism between the French tyrant's rapier-like intellectual faculty and his ultimately doomed romantic compulsion, points to the more substantial later monographs on Erasmus and Calvin, and the popular biographies of Marie Stuart, Magellan or the unfinished Balzac. In the essay on Ypres, one of the most assured here, Zweig lays out his pacifist credentials in no uncertain terms. The section 'Jamboree upon the Dead' echoes the more acerbic attack by fellow Austrian Karl Kraus, in his 'Promotional Trips to Hell' (1921), which one feels Zweig must have read. Kraus' eruption of contempt for the tourism and media hyenas who profit from the leftover carcass of the war, offering their 'battlefield tours' with every luxury and comfort afforded the visitor, is commendable. Today such a scenario would be an obscenity so overt it would not be tolerated; and yet, if one travels to the immaculately restored, 'dummy' Ypres of today, one still finds curios in shop windows made of spent shells similar to those that Zweig remarks on, one still finds tour groups and coaches spilling their contents onto the now perfectly restored cloth hall square. If the promotional fanfare is less audible, the behaviour of visitors more solemn, the secret thirst for ticking off significant sites and purchasing mementoes of the genocide of Europe's youth seems unquenched.

Zweig's clear hatred of authoritarianism, of dogma, of orthodoxies, of senseless inequalities, of basic unfairness, come through in all his essays, but in none more strongly than 'Ypres'. His impression of the Menin Gate is genuinely moving, even though it may seem to us now over polite, rather too earnest. Likewise the account of the venerable old Zurich hotel lost to developers, a tale reminiscent of his despairing friend Joseph Roth's brief but terribly poignant piece on the closing of his beloved Hotel Foyot in Paris in 1938. But perhaps most telling of Zweig's growing preoccupation with humanity's behaviour faced with nationalist barbarism are the final essays written during the period of Zweig's exile in London. 'House of a Thousand Fates' (1937) is concerned with a shelter for Jewish vagrants that Zweig encounters in London. Of course, post-Holocaust, the pathos of this piece is almost intolerable. We read with the knowledge of what was to come and this honourable shelter becomes a helpless structure fixed at the point of being swept away in a nuclear blast of exterminatory zeal. And yet we read Zweig's careful inventory of humanity's potential for unselfishness, the tireless Sisyphus-like labour of this little volunteer-run shelter that relieves those who are fortunate to pass through it, at least for a time, of the anxieties wrought on them by their insecure situation. But in his essay on the London shelter, Zweig is not concerned with Jewishness, he is concerned with ordinary people who through no fault of their own have been victimised, he is concerned with their fate, with fundamental fairness and the small, sometimes all-but-lost hope that can perhaps evolve into the greater one, that can properly anchor when people come together and do what is right in human terms. That is what this shelter epitomises for him: an endangered decency, a dogged labouring back towards a state of mutual trust, in the face of insane persecution. In 'Gardens in Wartime' it is the composure of the English people Zweig wonders at, in their most challenging hour, as they calmly tend their allotments and patches of garden. This he compares to the frenzied atmosphere of the previous world war, when people charged forward in paroxysms of blind enthusiasm for the great adventure. With his customary generosity of spirit, Zweig hails the mysteriously calm, resigned-to-be war-yoked English as the victors, not necessarily of the war but of the way to live inside the machine of war and still remain connected to the natural world, to be human.

Although it might be tempting for mischievous detractors to accuse Zweig of imbuing his subject with a sometimes aesthetically rhetorical romanticism, I think such a knee-jerk reaction belies the genuine satisfaction to be had from these surprisingly dense yet delicately nuanced pieces, which show themselves furtively, like gentle landscapes that can often harbour more poetic colouring than dramatic ones. Zweig secures an image of a vanished period in a certain moment of its activity, a moment frozen during a fete or a fair, a station in the early morning coming to life, a moment of flowering or decline, the precise flavour of which we can never reclaim. Zweig has his aesthetic roots in the nineteenth century, among that stable of exemplary mood-discerners distilled from the symbolist movement. Not for nothing does he quote lines from the poet of Bruges, Georges Rodenbach, and not for nothing did he feel such a natural bond with Rilke, a poet habitually obsessed by the aesthetic, who in his turn revered Verhaeren and was significantly influenced by Rodenbach's melancholy verses. These travel essays are valuable bone fragments contributing to the overall skeletal remains of a European writer's journey through a period whose dizzying descent from security to chaos we simply cannot fully comprehend today. They show a man who was above all wilfully curious and unable to rest, a man who must write in order to exist, but travel to fully live. And one should be careful not to sigh complacently when noting another outburst of superlatives, of joy, or rapture, which pepper Zweig's earnest reactions, since the underlying current throughout, as in all his writings, is an innate awareness of loss. But Zweig is an instinctive activist against loss, a fighter for memory if preservation fails, his writings stained with the sense that time is running out both for him and for his generation. And this is clear decades before the appearance of that final celebrated compendium of remembrance, *The World of Yesterday*. In the end one is left with the sense that Zweig is the quarry, the man out of his time; that the ground between him and his hunters, whether they be overt or obscure, is continuously diminishing as he criss-crosses Europe's railways, as if endeavouring somehow to stitch the uncooperative continent together.

This sense of the imminent loss of individual freedom, the looming nimbus of totalitarianism and the herd's coming of age, is never more clear than in the essay 'To Travel or be Travelled', where Zweig witnesses the birth of mass tourism with such natural disdain. This essay represents a kind of proto-manifesto of inwardness, on what it means to be a solitary traveller and not a tourist. It still holds perfectly true today. Though we know Zweig's fears for the future of mass travel have been realised in the most decisively hopeless and depressing manner, we can still, as we embark on a journey alone, find against all the odds a certain enabling stoicism of the spirit in his words. Even if only for the celebration of that indecipherable inner fortification afforded by independent travel, one should read these invaluable essays, handed down to us by a man who ultimately was unable to contemplate living on in a world where such freedoms were consciously obliterated.

Travel must be an extravagance, a sacrifice to the rules of chance, from daily life to the extraordinary, it must represent the most intimate and original form of our taste. That's why we must defend it against this new fashion for the bureaucratic, automated, displacement en masse, the industry of travel.

Let us preserve this modest gap for adventure in a universe of acute regulation. Let us not hand ourselves over to these overly pragmatic agencies who shepherd us around like goods, let us continue to travel in the way our ancestors did, as we wish, towards the goal we ourselves have chosen. Only that way can we discover not only the exterior world but also that which lies within us.

A note on the texts

This selection of travel essays is taken from the collection *Auf Reisen*. From a considerable body of works I have chosen what I felt to be a representative selection of Zweig's writings on Europe. I have endeavoured to give some diversity in terms of period and place, and to present essays that I felt would engender most interest. I wished to avoid a glut of notes, so as not to encumber the reader travelling through these texts, therefore those notes that do exist were deemed worthy of inclusion for their particular instructive value, and when I felt the reader's understanding of the text may have been diminished by their absence. Zweig tended to pepper his essays with phrases from foreign languages; taking his lead, where such phrases appear in the text I have left them untranslated, though translations are provided in the notes. These phrases, a number of them English, are differentiated by being presented in bold, italic type. My aim was to render these texts in such a way that the distinctive tone of Zweig's language would be safeguarded as much as is reasonably possible, while at the same time making them accessible to the contemporary English reader. The photographs at the end of the volume present a number of Zweig's destinations in their current condition, as captured by me on my own journeys.

– Will Stone, 2010

Journeys

The Season in Ostend

The season in Ostend signifies a colourful and unbroken alternation of festivals and public events. For all who frequent this, the largest and most elegant among the Belgian coastal resorts, the motivation, officially at least, is that which otherwise incites most people to visit bathing resorts: the need for peace and relaxation. The person who, through the course of a year, has the sense of being dragged through the stimulating and thrilling round of metropolitan pleasures, who feels the pulse of life and all their resilience stretched to the limit and is, one might say, bloated with culture and refinement, becomes accustomed to profiting from summer weeks of harmonious relaxation in the calm contemplation of nature cut off from these energies. But for the clientele of Ostend it's different. For them, this summer lt is not a rest, a chance to switch off, on the contrary it's only another shining link in the endless chain of society distractions, an ersatz for the broiling boulevards of the metropolis, for their theatres, their festivals, their gardens, which summer renders unapproachable. Little by little Ostend has become the unofficial rendezvous-location for the real and bogus aristocracy that one sees floating like a spume above the waves of capitals, everywhere encountering and recognising itself, and for whom a home-town is merely a station in transit from which they seek to reach the great international centres of pleasure. Ostend shelters these welcome guests in high summer, from July to the last days of August.

One could speak copiously and endlessly of these days without ever evoking by a single word the happy situation of Ostend, for in the overall canvas, nature is merely a backdrop. You might say that here nature is only so prodigious in beauty in order to glorify the triumph of modern civilisation and to provide a frame worthy of its perfection, where within is celebrated human beauty and mankind's conquests in ingenuity. Here, the effect of the shore does not depend on the view extending into the distance over the sea, which bears to you a tangy and health-giving air, so much as on admiring the extraordinary elegance of the hotels on the front and the splendid outfits of the women gathered there as if they were promenading in the city. The pier, which runs far out into the sea, signals the great achievements of modern technology, the port with its elegant steamships and yachts; the beach is of more interest for the particular style of the bathing costumes and the rather prodigious display of freedom of manners, than through any effect of its own. As has been said, here nature is modest in comparison with the works of men, for culture comes to stand facing her, all-conquering with its last, most important and most refined achievements.

The physiognomy of Ostend is naturally the exact mirror of its visitors. People most active throughout the year feel in summer the need for idleness; on the other hand, those without profession, or whose jobs do not detain them, always aspire to some superficial occupation that they may satisfy here through sport or gambling. One fact proves to what extent gambling has become for Ostend a condition of existence: last year when the gaming rooms had to be closed at Ostend and Spa, the Belgian state wanted to award these two towns a compensation package of seven million francs – a decree that for the moment has not come to bear. In any case, the amount of compensation gives a rough idea of the astonishing level of receipts that each season's gambling gives rise to.

The centre of Ostend's world of elegance is the Kursaal. This splendid and substantial edifice stands alongside the sea wall, flanked on both sides by rows of the most elegant villas offering a view from the rear over Léopold Park and the town. In the great room, afternoons and evenings, the distinguished public of Ostend attend concerts; particularly in the evening when the men may only appear in society dress or dance attire, and women of all nations compete in the magnificence of their outfits and jewellery, when the vast room is filled to capacity by the noble ranks of the beau monde – and this is true even of the *demi monde* – in such moments Ostend leaves a veritably grandiose impression, even on the inhabitants of a major city. Every day after the concert they give a ball; but the majority of visitors retire then to the other rooms at the rear of the casino, which form part of the assembly rooms. In the first the gambling is public and open to all; of course, here the turnover is not so high and the most audacious bid for Red or Black is fixed at three hundred francs. Gambling properly speaking takes place at Cercle Privé, the biggest club in Ostend, which nevertheless does not operate a rigorous admissions policy and requests a mere twenty francs for the price of entry. There unfold the most interesting scenes, which from the very next day are customarily the talk of the town; losses and wins of several thousand francs at Roulette. The most sumptuous outfits mix together, sometimes belonging to real princesses, sometimes to princesses of the music hall; one encounters here also numerous cosmopolitan people of whom no one knows anything other than that they frequent all the world's casinos and are never absent so long as the gaming rooms remain open. And this scene continues, unchanged, from morning until the dawn of the following day.

Amongst the wealth of other distractions, it's as well to mention first the floral festivals where taste, wealth and beauty rise equally to the challenge of competition. This season they have been a little modified in relation to previous years. One can only view them in closed-off streets that require an entry fee to be visited. They have, for this reason, lost their ancient splendour, for then the whole town took part with great passion in the confetti-and-flower battle whose sphere spread to virtually all the elegant streets. Now, it's true, the procession of cars so pompously decorated wins in privacy, the struggle breathes an atmosphere of greater noblesse and one no longer experiences those untoward excesses that, in recent years, had distanced the distinguished public. In any case, the competition for the most beautiful car and the most attractive balcony obtained the most favourable results.

Naturally sport is never out of place in Ostend. Car races alternate with yacht and track races, pigeon shooting and dog racing, and no day passes when the Englishman in particular is not afforded the opportunity of placing a bet. The best attended are the horse races where they distribute winnings to a total value of four hundred thousand francs; especially during the Grand Prix d'Ostende, the composition of the public offers a marvellous spectacle as, for the grand occasions, they are not recruited exclusively from the ranks of health-resort visitors but also from the reunion of a sporting elite coming from nearby Brussels or London and even Paris. In the course of these days, on which the king himself is accustomed almost always to attend, Ostend deploys all her splendour, gathering beneath her sceptre the millions of diverse nations, their beauties, and for grandiosity only the nocturnal festivals can compare, when the sea and port, normally plunged in a profound darkness, are ablaze with a thousand coloured lights, and out of the night rockets shoot towards the sea wall flooded with an enchanted light from the projections of the lighthouse.

But trump card of the season must go to the great procession of officers. Requests for inclusion pour in from virtually all armies and this spectacle must certainly count among the most interesting of the year. Then comes September and with it little by little the bright colours fade. The hotels close up; Ostend, the town of Ostend, reveals itself more and more: the fishermen who scratch a living from their catch, the port from which boats leave for London or Holland, and primarily the poverty and destitution that usually, dazzled by glitter and luxury during the season, one does not notice. The summer residence of King Léopold of Belgium (who satisfies his predilection for cosmopolitan resort life, summer months in Ostend and winter months on the Côte d'Azur, and last season gave the honours to a very exotic guest, the Shah of Persia) closes its doors too and lowers its awnings, like all hotels whose activity ceases with summer's end. The freshening wind of autumn blows in off the North Sea. Then eight or nine sad months, where all rests in leaden sleep, until it starts all over again, this unique unforgettable game, of human fallibility, passions and distractions, which, each year, find themselves assembling for the season in the Belgian seaside resort.

– 1902

Bruges

It's hard to wander in the evening through the dark and confined streets of this dreaming town without abandoning oneself to a serene melancholy, that gentle nostalgia aroused by the last days of autumn; no longer the shrill feasts of the fruiting season, but the more restful drama of decay and natural forces in decline. Carried by the uninterrupted wave of the pious carillon of vespers, one gradually sinks into this boundless ocean of enigmatic memories that cling to every door and wall gnawed away by time. One is a casual pilgrim here, until suddenly sensing all the greatness of a drama where action and life seem to arise from one's own muffled footsteps, while mighty silent shapes are stood in the dark wings. No other town possesses a greater power to symbolise the tragedy of death, and perhaps even more terrifying the actual death throes, than does Bruges.

One fully experiences this in these half-convents, Béguinages, where many aged persons come to die, because what the austere contours of the streets in the evening can only leave us guessing at, reveals itself here through those weary glances, shunning any radiance, in which only a feeble ray of life reflects: that here is an existence without hope or prospect for the future, apathetic and entirely concerned with the past. One cannot easily forget the way of life of these folk who regard so impassively the shy blooming of the little convent gardens and show not the slightest interest in strangers. Equally astonishing is that crepuscular image of streets both ancient and empty.

And it's a strange thing: here, silence is not only linked to evening, which weaves about it all those dreams and nostalgic memories, but seems to spread constantly over the gabled roof-tops a veil of grey that draws into itself all sound and matter; muteness that distils noise into a murmur, outbursts of joyfulness into smiles and cries into sighs. Of course there can't be a total absence of hustle and bustle in the streets around midday. Barrows and carts trundle over the cobbles, people go about their business in order to earn their daily crust, numerous cafés, restaurants and estaminets bear witness to the care taken to maintain an agreeable foothold on this earth, and yet neither the inhabitants nor the town are smiling. Nowhere that gaiety characterised by the Flemish towns, gangs of children who sing and dance making their clogs ring out behind the Barbary organ grinder, nowhere the lavish garments in bold colours. And always these stifled sounds. When one ascends the cool and dark spiral staircase of the belfry, rooted, immense, inflexible on the marketplace like the giant Roland, and faintly oppressed by the weighing darkness, one encounters with a mix of fear and rapture the light spreading its luminous colours and one is bound to note that, down below within a boundary where activity reigns supreme, the human voice is absent. Of the town stretched out at your feet and of its charming setting only a gentle hum rises up, magic as the sound of the bells of Vineta above the sea on Sundays.[1] And this confusion of red tiled roofs, these indented gables and these window ledges of gleaming white give the impression in their disorder of being mere playthings cast aside by a casual hand amongst the greenery. Enchanted yet lifeless – that's how it seems, this entanglement of tightly crammed dwellings and circular cloisters, skilfully interspersed with modest plots occupied by lush gardens and wide lanes leading into that prosperous land of Flanders where stand the great windmills, vital accessories of the Dutch landscape, their sails ever whirling round. Yet even from such a height where one enjoys the more amiable and playful aspects of the town, it is impossible to ignore that tragic gesture that better allows one to understand the muted sorrow of the streets; an arm stretched greedily towards the distant ocean, that broad canal by which the silted-up port seeks to reach the salutary waves. The dramatic history of Bruges returns to one via memory: the flourishing beginnings of a time when every ship owner set out his stall here, when hundreds of ships decked with flags crisscrossed the port, when kings humbly negotiated with aldermen, while queens admired with secret yearning the sumptuous finery of the burghers. Then the slow decline: long years of war, epidemics, conflicts and finally the fortune that withdrew at the same time as the sea, leaving her enclosed within her walls. This last is distant now, only a silver line on the horizon visible on a clear day. And the colours of the town have faded, only the heavy brocaded altar cloths have retained the flush of their ardent purple; otherwise she wears a nun's habit, and the perpetual clamour of the port, not to mention the din from the taverns crowded with drinkers, are silenced as never before. Suddenly one comes to understand the gesture of refusal by which Bruges, like her elder sister Ypres, isolated herself from all other towns, which at the sign of a dawning epoch drew to themselves all the powers and honours of culture. Whilst Antwerp, Hamburg, Brussels and other sister towns in their bellicose fervour brandished aloft the standard of life, Bruges-the-solitary became ever more muffled in her robe and cowl, withdrawing into the belt of her ancient walls. Remaining there, motionless and brooding across the centuries, entirely turned towards the past, she ended up resembling a great monk, whose imposing bearing inspired both melancholy and an infinite respect, replete with wonder and enchantment.

This feeling of the ephemeral, of the fickleness of every object, seizes all who observe the shadow of such a mighty past fall onerously upon Bruges, and who sense, through the permanence engendered in these walls and within the inhabitants themselves, that state of dependence on which religion is founded. The roads, with their innumerable monuments to the memory of long-vanished figures, represent a call to humility so powerful that those who have grown up subjected to this influence cannot hide away from faith. And so here the sublime is not reflected in the infinity of time but in God and the symbols of the Catholic Church. There reigns in this town a faith dark, austere and resilient like the very churches themselves, which stand before God, stark, unyielding, lacking the customary intricate ornament of the Gothic jagged edge or dainty pinnacles. Missals and pious images adorn the boutiques, almost without rest the carillon sound the call to prayer. At every moment nuns and monks pass furtively, greeting each other in subdued tones, dark, silent, hurrying, funereal at first sight like harbingers of death. But as they draw closer, watching over the long lines of children in their care, and you discover beneath the white caps or in the shadow of wide brims, calm gentle faces, then you realise that only the constant reminder of grandeur and death could be behind so immutable a gravity and could have etched such a coarse picture of life in these features. And tirelessly the bells ring out and statues of saints are leant against peaceful bridges. Yet even in the onerous darkness of this faith quivers a mystical purple light. There is the ardent celebration of great miracles, the profound tenderness of the Marian cult and that gentle poetry of sacred things that only the simplest men are destined to create in the naive passions of their piety. One can hardly forget the day when the reliquary adorned with precious stones, containing the saviour's blood, is carried solemnly out from the chapel, the bliss of prodigal grace causing a shimmering of exultation in the silent town that spreads over these people who can barely raise a smile for worldly things. Is it not enchanting to follow this route studded with names so soft, with such a peaceful aura: to pass along the incomparable Quai Rosaire, before the Sisters of Charity, Notre Dame, the Béguinage, St John's Hospital, to arrive eventually at the Minnewater, the lake of love? This is a pool of murky motionless water on whose bank leans, like a sleeping night watchman, a dark round tower. The sky seems to rest upon the black wavelets and white clouds scud overhead, as if messengers of paradise. What solemnity, what majesty love must have been endowed with in the eyes of these people for them to attribute such a name to these dreamy and seraphic surroundings.

In truth, it's difficult to imagine anything more possessed of sorrowful beauty than the canals of Bruges. Their image is deeply affecting and they move in silence, entirely lacking that prattling romanticism of the Venice canals, the whisper of the black gondolas in their nocturnal gliding, the glinting of moonlit daggers, clandestine trials, hidden doorways, lonely serenades – all those tired incidentals of novels from around 1830. Certain verses of Georges Rodenbach celebrate in perfect fashion their melancholy beauty and one recites them slowly while walking, as if they were the melody lurking at the very heart of these dark and shadowy waters. One thinks of the wistfully nostalgic elegy '*Au lieu des vaisseaux grands, qui agitaient en elles*',[2] delicate verses that seem to unite Rodenbach's oeuvre with Bruges to such an extent that one cannot approve enough of the painter for having chosen this dream landscape as the background for his portrait (in the Luxembourg).[3] But many other books, filled with gentleness, seriousness, solemnity, would be equally pleasurable to browse through on these embankments lined with stone, in the shade of the great chestnuts, dreamers themselves, appearing to reflect in the darkness of the ripples. For these canals do not speak, do not murmur; they do nothing but listen. Faithfully they bear the image of the houses that lean their crumbling, ivy-choked walls against them; they reflect the sad light of vaulted bridges and high towers unaware even of the shy lapping of shimmering wavelets. Not a sound. They are eternal darkness, but the sky is held in their black mirror and they bear horror and silence to this town, something of another world, transcendence, the luminescence of stars.

And between passing clouds that are reflected come from time to time the gentle processions of white swans, marvellous solemn creatures whose mystery both death and silence share equally. To see them glide radiant and dignified on these funereal waters produces an indescribable effect. What poet could ever imagine an antithesis as dazzling and harmonious as that created here by fortune? Though one may even contest fortune here, for certain legends tell the origin of these wild yet peaceable swans. One claims they represent expiation for the murder of a duke, according to another they are there to remind quarrelsome inhabitants of the veils that floated in times past, symbols of a power lost through its lightness. But it appears a futile effort seeking to impose on this astonishing beauty a will and a meaning, to drape it in the folds of legend.

For in this town of dream and death all gently tends, in its crepuscular light, towards mysticism. As Bruges already has something of the unreal about it, it is easy to weave around its buried history, into the depth of centuries, romantic arbours and flowery verse. That poetry, when it is braided about a real living figure, transforms it into legend, and often this threatens, however beautiful it might be, to embellish the reality. So it is that one of these moving tales touches the town's greatest creator spirit, Hans Memling, this pious man who only sought to confer on things a religious enchantment and to grant a reflection of the inaccessible, a yearning that caused a tremor through his soul. In spite of all the denials made by art history, here they still claim that Hans Memling, gravely wounded at the battle of Nancy, was cared for devoutly at the St John's Hospital and that in gratitude he painted the celebrated works – incomparable treasures – sheltered by this dilapidated building. Faintly oppressed by the permanent sorrow of the streets, I returned to see them, in order to savour through their grace brimming with freshness and their profound purity that perfume of springtime that seems impossible to locate in this town. They are all together in one little room – much more impressive gathered together than exposed in the gallery of the Flemish Primitives – a ray of light piercing the shroud spread over the town. It's hard to know which to favour: the Madonna who proffers an apple to the infant Jesus with an air so tender and grave, or else the so famous reliquary that tells with a piety that now seems child-like the legend of Saint Ursula. What a sensibility must have inhabited the soul of this artist – a soul that seems close to that other proclaimer of Bruges, Georges Rodenbach, but not so consciously filled with mellifluous visions and adrift in celestial love. Is it not possible then to accept the legend: this delicate being, wounded by life, arrives in a town, already so pious, and discovers between the walls of a convent the rapture of creation?

Before returning in the evening through the troubled streets of the silent town, I left the paintings to give a moment to the hospital itself. One reaches it via a narrow courtyard, passing between statues of saints that seem to incline. Here are laid out little flowerbeds of fragile blooms, listless. From the cool corridors one notices behind the grey curtains the neat rows of white beds. Here, too, a silence oppresses. Nuns in their white caps glide soundlessly. In the garden a few convalescents in long grey hospital robes, women resting and children playing. Here and there a few luminous patches of the late sun. The children were hardly noisy; however they leapt, trying to catch one another, while the convalescents followed them with an expression of ardent curiosity that only life caught in perpetual rebirth may grant. And when I listened, after so many hours of silent wandering, to this clear and silvery childish laughter – resonant even within the walls of the dead – I experienced a feeling of joy. I was seized with a faint anguish about the notion of returning to this sepulchral town whose symbols embraced me with such power that I felt an infinite pity for these people who lived here in the shadows, inexorably on the path towards death, towards the incomprehensible. Rarely had I felt with such intensity that hackneyed wisdom contained in the alphabet, according to which death must be signally mournful while life is an interminable force that compels even the most recalcitrant to love.

– 1904

The City of Popes

Rarely does an impression impose itself so potently, so forcefully, so directly, as the sight of Avignon: here reigned powerful men. If other towns possess their proud edifices, often only a plan or symbol of their ancient overlord, nowhere does the insignia of imperious rule express itself with such vigour as in the city of popes. The entirety of this charming Provençal town extends informally and peacefully along the deep blue of the Rhone, a marvellous landscape that nature's goodness grants a profound mildness and captivating beauty. But, above the white roofs, which blaze and shimmer in the burning sun, above this white sea of foam and spray stands proud and commanding a colossal rock, stark, savage, sheer walls, the palace, or more precisely, the castle of the popes. And like bars of stone are the raised ramparts encircling this town, still intact today in spite of assault and conflict. The broad arch spanning the Rhone, built in 1177 by St Bénezet and almost turned into a fortress by the popes, is broken and now from the middle of the river stares emptily at the opposite bank. One senses it: that these indestructible walls were at one time the result of the most embittered struggles, during the epoch of the three popes, who waged war using not only excommunication but also weapons and castles – that period of prodigious natural forces whose brutality harmonised with the artistic during the Renaissance, to herald the appearance of its most illustrious figures.

Avignon acquired this historical importance at the time when the popes, chased out of Italy, sought a homeland in France. Those hundred years saw the construction of this colossal citadel, made necessary both by the precarious situation facing the stateless popes, always harassed by new enemies, and the lack of natural defences of a town situated in a low-lying area.

Ever higher, ever stronger the ring became, an impregnable town of refuge, the safest home for the diadem. And when the popes returned to Rome, the antipopes took up residence in this eyrie, and not until the fifteenth century did Avignon become a peaceable episcopacy of the Roman church, which it remained until the bloody days of the French Revolution. Yet, despite centuries of tranquillity, Avignon has preserved intact the character of its warlike past.

As in all towns of a certain size, reality leaves one with a feeling of disillusionment at the sight of its great historic monuments. Today the fortress of the popes is a French barracks: in the hatch openings you notice laughing faces beneath red caps; in the courtyards, indignant officers command hordes of recruits. But the dimensions are too imposing for the sensation of the grandiose to be lost – it suffices merely to observe these several-metre-thick walls, these high towers from whose flat terraces prisoners were simply hurled into the horrific abysses during the years of the Revolution. And the church of Notre Dame, at the heart of the fortress, from whose clock tower the golden form of the holy Virgin radiates out and for a few hours blazes across the country working her mediating ways. She shelters the tomb of Jean XXII, a narrow, slender rising monument of white stone lacking portrait or inscriptions. From the church one takes a path through a verdant garden to a wide terrace, from which one embraces the blossoming landscape. And there one can properly understand the love of the popes for this residence, for this impregnable castle where they could enjoy in peace all the charms of a southern spring. Broad and blue flows the Rhone beneath, her numerous bends dividing the radiant countryside from the far distance and enclosing – at the foot of the castle – the little isle of Barthelasse. Beneath, the white sea of roofs shines, the battlements of the church tower greet you fraternally; a panorama splendid above all for the clarity and purity of its colours, the azure of the sky. On the opposite bank is the fort St-André, immense construction of the fourteenth century, which stares back at you, presiding over both the new town and the Avignon fortress. In the distance gleams the tower where fires were lit to maintain contact between the old town and the popes' palace, to enable protection from attack. One can barely imagine anything more lovely than this spectacle on a day in early spring when the colours of the fields do not yet quite merge exactly with the purer green of the always verdant gardens and the landscape frees itself with keen lines against a clear cool sky.

The town offers still more treasures: the myriad views allowing one to seize with ever renewed surprise the splendour of the region; the old churches, like St-Pierre, St-Didier, Val-de-Bénédiction, that have faithfully preserved the artistic style of their origins (around the early thirteenth and fourteenth centuries – precisely the epoch of the popes' interregnum), and not forgetting the charming image of a small modern Provençal city worming its way more and more between the ancient monuments. But another tender memory relates to Avignon – even though it reaches beyond its walls: the famous Fontaine de Vaucluse, immortalised by those two great figures of love, Laura and Petrarch. Don't people go to Avignon just to be shown the place in the church where the poet encountered his beloved for the first time? Of what immense interest they are then, these authentic historical locations of their love, where Petrarch the renowned scholar composed a great number of his marvellous sonnets. If the source itself is not particularly memorable, its romanticism is not entirely unworthy of Petrarch, who made it unforgettable: in a green ravine, clasped between rocks, the water suddenly leaps like a white flame to descend in a roaring cascade down the valley, clear, transparent, a truly invigorated spring. On white roads one makes again for Avignon, leaving behind one beauty for another, the scene of a great love for the Provençal landscape, the country of the most tender courtly ballads and the knight poet's escapades, for the genuine landscape of spring.

– 1905

Arles

In fact Arles is a true provincial town, small and difficult to find one's way around with its narrow, irregular and barely sanitary streets: one of those places that leaves such a charming impression when viewed from a railway carriage – a toy in the distance, charming and colourful – but which loses its attraction as soon as one draws near. In economic terms it has no importance. Even during the period when the rail network was being constructed in Provence some had wanted to leave it to one side, but a number of French poets succeeded, thanks to their own intervention, in establishing the connections that enabled the true worth of the legendary historical treasures gathered together in this little town to be recognised. Frédéric Mistral, the famous re-awakener of Provençal poetry whose name, since he won the Nobel Prize, we now hear often, founded a national museum, the musée Arlaten, fated to become in some sense a centre for the promotion of Provençal culture. However, the principal service rendered by the poets to this little town was to sing the praises of its women: Mistral, Daudet and the composer Bizet thus proclaimed to the world the grace of the Arlésiennes. And no less than in another age, during the period of prosperity when she was known as Arelate, the Arles of today basks in universal renown.

Yes, narrow filthy lanes. But then suddenly a vast square opens before one and a colossal construction commands the attention. The Roman amphitheatre, probably the greatest of ancient Gaul, designed to hold some thirty thousand spectators, looms up with its imposing sphere, the richness of its façades, the luxuriance of its ornament. It once, as depicted in a medieval engraving, sheltered within its walls the entire town of Arles, so grandiose are its dimensions. It was only in 1825 that for aesthetic reasons they undertook the demolition of the little houses that had often been erected from the old stones and the reconstitution of the ancient space (in the same way that, in nearby Orange, the ancient theatre has been transformed into a modern arena). Certainly, these days it continues to fulfil its former function, the regular staging of bullfights on summer Sundays, yet these festivities are only a pale substitute for the splendour that must once have graced these terraces, judging from the magnificence of the edifice. For in the second century Arles was under the rule of Constantine, a native son, and then his successors, one of the beacons in a Roman Empire encompassing the whole of Europe. But simultaneously, in its capacity as seat of the archbishop, Arles was a centre of the Catholic Church, which had also left it a legacy of precious monuments. The great migrations mark the beginning of its decline, occasionally interrupted by brief periods of prosperity, such as the crowning of Charles Quint who declared himself King of Arles. Little by little it fell into obscurity and one had to wait for the word of the poets to awaken its name, if not the town itself.

The most evident trace of Rome's splendour is to be found in the theatre, of which alas we possess little more than a few vestiges. Her most precious treasures have been displaced, such as the famous *Venus of Arles*, which was offered in 1683 to Louis XIV and is today one of the most valuable sculptures in the Louvre. Various finds have been reunited in the musée Lapidaire,[4] though they are likely to be of interest to qualified archaeologists only.

No less significant are the gifts made in the thirteenth and fourteenth centuries by the pontiff of the town. In honour of St Trophime, a Greek missionary sent, according to legend, by Peter himself to convert the Gauls to Christianity, a church was built and also cloisters exhibiting a supreme artistry. Here the legend continues to spin its colourful threads: at this location they erected a church to be sanctified by St Trophime in person, the first dedicated to the glory of the mother of God and her eternal life. Here stands one of the most beautiful Romanesque cathedrals in all Provence, sublime above all for its doorway, whose architectural work can only be compared to that of the church of St Gilles. A few steps on and we are led to the cloisters which, with the coolness of their vaulted passages and their wide capitals, arouse an impression of infinite respect.

But the place that has made the Arles of another age into one of the most famous sites in the world is the Alyscamps, the Elysian Fields, ancient necropolis for all of Christianity. St Trophime was originally interred there and soon word spread that the ground thus consecrated was the location of an abundance of signs and miracles. By contact with it they believed the body was protected, primarily from all diabolic influence; and so rapidly it became throughout the entire Christian Western world a labour of devotion to procure for the dear deceased a plot at the Alyscamps. It was enough to simply let the coffin be carried down the Rhone, unaccompanied, to reach its pious destination. Princes, dukes, bishops and wealthy merchants arranged to be buried there, the number of tombs rising to several thousand. Like Ariosto, Dante evokes this necropolis in his *Divine Comedy*. Not until the miraculous remains of St Trophime were transferred to Marseilles did the cemetery lose its importance. Today all that's left is a narrow avenue between lofty willows, flanked on left and right by plain open sarcophagi; the most precious, mainly those of princes, were exchanged by the Arlésiens in the seventeenth century against coin of the realm. Some boats that Charles IX had loaded with coffins foundered in the Rhone; the remaining valuable examples are preserved in the musée Barberini in Rome. All that endured was the inconspicuous little chapel.

To fill the vast expanse separating this glorious distant past and the present is the purpose of the musée Arlaten founded by Frédéric Mistral. It contains paintings, handicrafts and costumes of authentic medieval Provence, souvenirs of a country, such as Mistral's cradle, and many a pretty trifle. Yet no other curiosity does the foreigner go to more effort to see, as long as he prefers the splendour of life to ancient stones, than the spectacle of the Arlésiennes, so famed for their beauty. But here he may be obliged to suffer a slight deception. For Parisian fashion, or more exactly the provincial store, has banished the regional dress almost entirely across the whole area. And if one sometimes encounters one of those tall silhouettes of the classical kind mildly tempered by southern climes, it still rankles that the poets have awoken in us an expectation that has not been fulfilled. This slight exaggeration should not surprise us: indeed, if the women of Arles were really the most beautiful in the world, as their bards claim, then today instead of being a solitary visitor there, one would be merely a pilgrim in the midst of a crowd of curious onlookers.

— 1905

Springtime in Seville

There are towns where one is never present for the first time. You stroll through their unknown streets yet everywhere you feel as though you are encountering memories, you have the impression of being hailed by kindred voices. Their faces – for towns can be like men, sad and old, smiling and young, menacing and slender, lithe and worn – you may know from a sister town, or from an image, a book, a song, a dream. And Seville is like that. In some sense it is both likeable and familiar. All at once the name of Salzburg comes to mind. And not only in the name of Mozart, in nimble Figaro's character, in tender melodies do these two distant cities hold a pleasurable association. In stature and voice, in nature and behaviour they have a sisterly connection. They both possess such a powerful poetic that whatever is provincial in them takes on a charming and desirable character, and the horrible modern street culture does not impose itself so brutally, but joins forces and adapts itself tactfully to the ancient buildings. The nature of ancient nobility is in them; slender like page boys are the clock-towers and the bright bells have the freshness of girls' voices. All resonates brightly in the luminous streets, like a smile secreted in the green of the town. However, one should not forget that in the south, the image is much softer and more opulent; palms with green fans line the streets year-long and the colourful abundance of a splendid flora drops down to the gardens and avenues of the town. Music, with which both are saturated, has in Salzburg at least distilled two or three great masterworks: the tomb of Michael Haydn and the cradle of Mozart appear to be the point of calm around which life vibrates. In Seville, the sense of music does not take permanent form, but all the lanes resound with it, both good and bad, the air is perpetually alive with the humming of ditties, or the twang of a guitar. Here, life seems to have a quickened cadence and one could say the people a more lively blood in them; nowhere does one find more starving bellies than in Andalusia and yet in the splendour of her fervent colours, Seville shines cheerfully and gestures with her numberless flags that here one can truly be happy.

Is this really the Spanish character? Yes and no. For Spain only constitutes a unity on the map; in fact it is cut into two parts that schematically oppose each other and then, in their turn, dissolve into a thousand contrasts. The Spain of Pizarro and the Torquemada is still alive here,[15] the dark and fanatical Castilian spirit extends the arrogant cruelty of its art into new forms. These are not guitar players who inhabit the gloomy and decayed towns of the north, grey Toledo, which with the enclosure of its walls is suspended menacingly within the rock, where the furious Tagus passes through; these are the monks of another age and those great severe men, through whom the drab and mournful land-scape, with its sheer and stubborn rock-faces, achieved a semblance of life. But only a semblance: there is something sepulchral in many of the ancient towns, something of the monastic about their inhabitants. It is enough to think of Seville, of the waves of joyfulness that roll in, especially during carnival days, to properly sense the full horror that in the north of Spain hides itself behind welcome distractions. Right to the heart of Madrid, the fashionable city, the evil exhortation. As in our own Prater there is a procession in Buen Retiro; but where is the brisk and supple movement of the horses, the bright sound of their clip-clopping and the roar of their gallop, where are these colourful images of a restrained urgency? Wide, ponderous, in a state of half-dreaming the great coaches clatter past, extraordinarily erect, dignified and correct. Atop the coaches uniformed servants trimmed with braid are rigidly set, with the fanatical eyes of the monks of Zurbaran. Hard falls the shadow of the Escorial[16] over the entire Castilian landscape. Arriving in Andalusia one has the impression of emerging from this shadow into the sun. The contrast, so dazzling, is reflected in a hundred different mirrors. There it is the Spain of *Don Carlos*, *The Jew of Toledo*, and the *Torquemada* of Victor Hugo, visions of menacing savage beauty. And Seville? You begin by looking for the cheerful shop of 'Barbier', equally you have a wish to discover among the many gleaming houses the one where Don Juan undertook the adventure that Lord Byron tells of with such enchanting elaboration in his epic poem. Figaro sings his airs here, the 'Habanera' of Carmen warbles away, a symbol of merriment art has brought to these streets, through which passed once the ingenious hidalgo Don Quixote de la Mancha on his valiant Rossinante. Here one does not buy daggers for souvenirs, as in Toledo, but guitars and castanets. Seville is not the symbol of Spain, but it is Spain's smile.

Even war has led to reconciliation here. Of course the Moors eventually left the south of Spain following five centuries of colossal struggle – tears in their eyes, as legend would have it – and yet their nature is still felt everywhere through a secret life. Not held in contempt as in Castile, on the contrary their art is utilised here. And their greatest achievement, their art of life, that lethargic, sensual and voluptuous way of enjoyment, is so marvellously in accord with the joyous Andalusian lifestyle. This reconciliation appears across a hundred buildings. Mosques have become churches; the Giralda, that delightful and slender minaret, today sends its flight of bells piously down to the cathedral that crowds in on it. But it's in the houses that the union is most ingeniously stimulating. It's true they are in the Moorish style, low and bare, with flat roofs and rectangular courtyards. But here mystery and darkness have given way to gaiety. Windows and balconies are breaches in the Arabs' enclosed walls and allow light into the rooms. Bright and gleaming too is the paintwork, and never is the door closed with anxiety. At the end of passage-ways that beam cheerfully, covered with their coloured ceramics, one's gaze falls on the patio, the interior courtyard, where a jet of water surrounded by palms and dark shrubs splashes the flowers with a light spray. Even the poorest house has its flowers; even in the ancient ghetto where the house of Murillo stands, the colourful tufts shine out. From the balconies long garlands fall to the street below; in cheerful rows, like brightly coloured soldiers, avenues traverse the entire town. A wonderful palette of colours is displayed here, for the green wave breaks through into even the most miserable streets and everywhere the flowers send out their spray of sparks. But they burn all the same – like the coal in a dark oven – in the hair of girls, fiery carnations and red roses, worn with pride and tenderly safeguarded.

And even the women, entirely adorned with flowers, have something of the fugitive beauty of these blooms within them. Often they appear from a distance like flowers themselves in their garish dresses and in the flickering billowing of their mantillas, which give them such an inimitable manner. One thinks of the quivering of flower stems when admiring their supple step, of the gentle swaying of stalks in the wind's caress, this tempting sway, this secret dance. All the ardour of the sun seems to beam from their gaze, which, in a lightning flash, brushes against the onlooker, but – alas, as Théophile Gautier has remarked – *'Une jeune Andalouse regardera avec ses yeux passionnés une charrette qui passe, un chien, qui court après sa queue.'*[17] Even in moments of indifference do they exhibit that impassioned air that emanates from the flash of a look and the involuntary voluptuousness of their movements. And just as their language does not transform into a song, but without weariness or exertion turns towards it, so likewise dance spontaneously detaches from their round gestures, from their swaying gait. One must have seen the flamenco in the shabby cafés to know just how unattractive and schematic the rusty gestures of our ballet are, those that rest on a certain number of lazzi learnt by heart, whose enrichment is only possible through artificial embellishments. Here, dance is what it must be: an art form, finding its origin almost naturally in the graceful movements of the body, gestures of desire and rhythmical arousal; an art not of the legs, but emerging from the pleasure of the line, the curve of the back, a display of all possible forms of human beauty. All the little symbols of femininity are put to use in this dance: the fan, the mantilla, the veil, and above all the dress, which moulds the movements, softens them and expands them. Most of these dancers have only superficial training and the purely plastic gestures displayed by a good number of them at the start of their performance are really quite monotonous. But when roused by the clacking of the castanets, the sensuality of these gipsy dancers rises, wild yet not lascivious; a force frees itself from this ardour and seizes you so the blood surges through your veins, a magical frenzy, music of bewitchment, the wildness of the föhn.[18] Because of its human effect, such a dance is here again awarded the rank of art, while at home it is merely labelled amusement; it lies closer to our sensibility because it is nourished by passion and beauty, by the purely primitive and not by stylised expressions of life. Therefore melody and song have for these dances only a secondary and insignificant role, rather like the prosaic Arabic verses that accompany songs. Only the Andalusian loves to provoke these lyrics with jocular punch-lines and to stress clearly the amorous moment. For Seville is still in some way the relaxed town of Don Juan, without pomp but fanatic in its piety, joyful but without severity in its morality. A charming legend tells of this better than anything else: above the door of the great tobacco manufacturer, through which each day enter and leave four thousand women workers, old and young, pretty and ugly, a stone angel stands, the Renowned, holding a trumpet. And the rumour is that the day when a virtuous girl steps across the threshold, the trumpet will sound. That has never happened, although the angel has held his trumpet patiently for five hundred years. Not only is Figaro immortal here but Don Juan also.

Behind these smiles, Seville is nevertheless guardian of a great and solemn past. In spite of the perhaps rather faded colours, the Easter festivals remain famous the world over, with their sumptuous processions and those strange customs from distant centuries. In light waves modern life invades, the ancient gold tower of the Moors now sees broad boats ascend the calm yellow waves of the Guadalquivir[19] and at the summit of the Giralda, there where in another age the muezzin called the faithful to prayer, an unforeseen spectacle awaits the observer. An illuminated town, dissolving far, far into the country, shines forth brilliantly with her marvellous gardens, her ribbon of vast roads inclining to the distance; scarcely can one take it all in. So opulent is this palette of colours, one understands that Velázquez and Murillo are children of this city whose beauty they forever declaimed, in the same way that Lope de Vega has, in his theatre, born witness to its history and the musicians reported its joy. Here is born the poet of whom the people are in need – a happy man, a free man, a wise mocker in the image of Cervantes, or a magician like the painters of Seville – since the town gives so much, the cheer of a colourful life, the rhythm of perpetual re-animation in its events and the allegro of inner merriment. Why would such a wonderful thing not occur in a place that is itself a wonder? '*Quien no ha vista Seville, no ha visto maravilla*'[20] – this proud aristocratic saying one hears until it becomes unbearable; and yet such vanity one can scarcely reproach. For is it not a miracle, when men and so many years of destiny reckon to build a town, and ultimately leave a smile drawn on the face of life?

– 1905

Hyde Park

Hyde Park in London, surely the strangest of the great city parks, is in the true sense of the word not beautiful. It lacks virtually everything that makes a garden a work of art. It is flat, poor, an English heath, only at the gates is there evidence it is a garden at all. But its beauty lies not so much in the clearly perceptible, but in what is unsaid. For example, there are a few places where one can relax completely. One stands upon a broad expanse of meadow with an unending incline to infinity, a stilled pond of greenery on which trees touched by a gentle breeze sway like moored ships. To right and left irregular avenues emerge without perspective, but withdraw softly into the grey wings of the fog. Silence breathes here, only a few people pass now and then. Only flocks of sheep that, chewing, pluck at the grass. One forgets all, for a moment, so all-encompassing is the surrounding calm. Where could one be? Is this the world-famous Lüneburg heath?[5] Or Cornwall, Lord Tristan's dark land; might the sorrowful melody of the shepherds suddenly rise up?[6] Powerfully then does one grasp the idea that these soft borders in the distance are giant blocks of houses, that this silent heath on left and right is surrounded by a city the size of Milan, Lyon or Marseilles. In the names of all these great cities are contained the two syllables of the word 'London'. The feverish vision of Verhaeren, those *villes tentaculaires*, which with arms like those of polyps absorb the green of the countryside and draw the heath-lands into the grey gelatinous mass of their stone – here in this cyclopean town such a wild hallucinated dream has become reality. Thousands of ships, arriving from distant oceans, converge on her, millions of hands toil for her, beneath the surface speed the underground lines, above the roofs, trains storm past, each year more and more houses spew into the greenery – and right in the middle of all that, as if lost in dream, a heath with bleating sheep, a silent peaceful sky all of its own, to which the wheezy breath of thousands no longer wells up. Like the beauty of London itself, that of Hyde Park resides in its disproportion.

No, Hyde Park does not at first glance overwhelm the on-looker. It's not in the nature of the English to open up to the foreigner so quickly, not in the nature of the people nor that of the landscape. One must first approach with love, to come to know the secret strangeness in the monotonous poverty that is this heath-land. Here the grass has a colour found nowhere else, the soft shade of early spring; the leaves, which fall only thinly, shine luminous with a silvery light. Then too, this landscape lies beneath the frosted glass pane of the English sky, where light is weakened and in the eternal play of veils all mysteries of the chiaroscuro unfold. Here the ether is a cold, almost leaden blue, when it is not crossed by clouds; the sunshine is not as in Italy, a glowing white bundle of light that burns down, blinding the stone, so much so that dazzled, terrified, it sends the embers back, but only a feeble flowing shimmer, soon captured by a cloud as if in a butterfly net. And here shadow is not a cold, black hiding place, a stark outline, but a grey clot above the grass. In terms of painting, Hyde Park has, in its daylight hours, the timid delicate colours of the Pre-Raphaelites, and when evening falls it encloses itself in the mystical vapours of a Carrière. And the air, which just as unwillingly bears sound, light, colour and groping glances, colours in a peculiar way this heavy London atmo-sphere, saturated with salt off the sea, made yellow by the mists and grey by the smoke of countless chimneys. It veils forms, makes them rounded and obscure, dims the distance and causes the sky close by to incline prematurely into the outline of the horizon's shadow. Between the trees at noon, it lets float a light bluish mist, like the smoke-curl from a cigarette; and in the evening, a greyish ash-like vapour that obscures everything,

Nibelheim opening his dark door.[7] A grey cloud glides over the city and heath, making people forget, for long weeks on end, that in the vault of the sky the eternal dance of glittering stars goes on. To compensate it draws, during daylight, wonderful smoke images at the borders of one's gaze; factories and houses for rent are lured into these grey quivering shadows like the mythical castles of the Holy Grail, all nuances of half darkness alleviating the austere and unpleasant forms of reality.

But all that does not make this park worthy of love. For this beauty is simply one of those things that lie beneath the heavens, pure and free, and are as it were closer to the secret source from where light and shadow stream, the gold of the sun and the smoke of the fog. It's simply the beauty of an area of English heath-land. But exactly: Hyde Park is a heath at the heart of a town, not so much a spectacle in itself as on the one hand the stage upon which a curious life unwinds, and on the other the stalls of relaxed spectators. Its true beauty is that of the people who bring it to life, of that marvellous race who apply themselves less to achieving gracefulness, than to strengthening healthy passions, in sport and games. And so to love the English it is not enough just to speak with them, one must be in real communication with them; one does not come to love them through a gentle stroll but in witnessing all those activities that are displayed here: running, jumping, riding, boating, bathing, games, in all their splendid, perfectly restrained strength. Hyde Park contains their whole life, as much of it as is not played out within four walls. In London the street is indeed entirely monopolised by commerce, it has no room for the spectacle of the *flâneur*, the adventurous loafing about of composed self-satisfaction. That's why all those who relish pleasure in a look or a movement seek refuge in the park, which receives them all, with its green arms outstretched to the infinite. Thus change breaks out in its dreamy calm, and yet there is something measured in these spectacles: something regular like the office timetable day by day, as if that constituted its real occupation, its 'business'.

This life begins early, very early. Often hazy clouds hang in the sky and the trees seem fluffed in cotton wool. Then a few bicycles murmur towards the pond, which smooth, motionless seems to be waiting for them, and lads, workers, schoolchildren gather on the bank. Promptly clothes are removed, cast on the sand, and naked bodies progress through the water with vigorous thrusts. Then they all rush over the grass, doing gym, boxing, letting the sun shine on their naked dew-streaked bodies, without supervision, without taxes, in complete freedom of nature, which in the hazy distance appears like some fairy wood. A marvellous moment of nature at the centre of a great city, which one hardly finds elsewhere, the luminous, unforgettable image, and one of the loveliest adventures one can experience in London. And then, at eight o'clock all is over and free bathing is forbidden until evening. But immediately other beautifully animated images take their place within the framework of the waking park. Fast rowers, bent and stretched again, bodies moving in rapid rhythm, their slender boats travel shimmering across the lake, a silent arrow, only the rudder flaps in smoothing movements above the water. Then come the first riders upon their splendid English horses; at the gallop they blast along the avenues, the human charges seeming to be of the same race of steel as their horses, lusty and intoxicated with their own might, foam sprayed right to the croup. So in this manner the morning is soon over, and the warm sun above makes the leaves shiver, a shimmering mist hovers above the heath. Then arrives that hour of calm that all gardens know around midday, that moment when the park seems to be the only one breathing, with flowers and grasses that spread open greedily, to drink in the sun. The people accommodated at this hour are silent: idly sprawled on the grass, like heavy fruits dropped from the trees; on benches reading newspapers a few superfluous people. All seems to be waiting in expectation for a great moment. And soon it arrives. The children storm across the grass from tables; girls with all the youthful strength of their slender agility hurl the ball from their slim wrists to one another; the boys who run wildly across the plain; the afternoon stroller with books and newspapers – this is all merely a prelude. Around four o'clock, it begins: from Piccadilly they come, to Hyde Park Corner, the long procession of carriages, this show of London's wealth, elegance and beauty, a theatre like those only offered by cities with a deeply rooted ancient culture, like Vienna during May days at the Prater and Madrid in the Buen-Retiro. What surprises here, however, are the number and diversity of types of carriage. Whereas in Vienna the light-springed hansom cab predominates and in Madrid the heavy bullock-trot of the solemn state coaches, here all manner of types flow together, which even for the layman proves a most attractive spectacle. One sees the heavy teams, so stiff and severe with their powdered lackeys you might think they had stepped out of an old engraving. Then once again the light bicycles speed past, automobiles whirr between them: all resound at the same beat of time, from the restrained step of the fiery horses that appears to make them feverish, to the express tempo at which a trained sportsman rushes his trotting steed through the crowd, exceeding all the other cars. But the most captivating is surely the curious form of the hansoms, so typical to London, which through the soft gliding silent movement and silhouette of the driver hunched above the black box somehow evoke the rocking motion of the Venetian gondola. Then there is the multitude of beautiful and beautifully framed portraits of people in relaxation and movement, the backwards leaning women observing around them, the upright drivers straight as candles, the seemingly frozen silhouette of the servant, the inquisitive children, and surrounding all in a gigantic circle, on chairs, the benevolent public, at whom this spectacle seems aimed. There is an extraordinary richness of light, colours and quick movements, lacking order and yet not restless, perpetually excited and yet not deafening. For this is the particular energy of this country, to soften even the most vivid tensions and to ensure the city's colossal system of gears is maintained on orderly rails, that silence breathes, as in the great machine houses, allowing the transformation of immense power on well-oiled cogs to be produced soundlessly. And this restraint appears to be inherited here, since the children – those delightful precociously silent children – have only a mute interest in the colourful game, which goes on all day until the evening. But peace has not yet fallen on the park. While the human tide little by little ebbs away, a mass of a quite different kind gathers at the other end by Marble Arch. Improvised speeches are delivered there – all have the right to speak about anything – and since England has never lacked for the sectarian one observes eccentric characters, often scruffy and dirty, expound their point of view, beneath a free sky, before those who are willing to listen. Unelected tribunes of the people, agitators for the most diverse ideas, they speak in the quivering light of a candle, stood on a stool; their fanatical words rise above the people towards the darkness that threatening seems already to descend from the crowns of the trees. Religious groups assemble their faithful and strike up hymns, whose mighty breath blows powerfully across the fading heath. Once more they come, liberated from work, the embers of its overheated warmth inflamed, the wild cries mingle, just as over there cars cross the commotion, quick as arrows, passing then immediately vanishing. And finally, when the moonlight and fog form a hanging web above the heath, then a last hum comes along, the evening finale of all parks: love. Entwined couples glide through the darkness, whispers quiver from a thousand different hideaways, the shadow seems to come alive and in passing one sees the often-audacious game of *ombres chinoises*.[8] The intertwining of melodies closes with a minor chord.

Thus the park lives day after day with the rhythm of an English man of commerce, who with circumspection grades and counts his hours. And as with every Englishman he has his Sunday off, when he sports the richly embroidered festive attire of so many people. After morning service, England's aristocratic society promenade in the 'church parade' along the great avenues, usually reserved for speeding vehicles, and whoever wishes to put a name to a face marked by indifference can have all the earls and counts coming and going pointed out to him by an obliging friend. In the afternoon Hyde Park shelters the masses, drawing them through its gates with blooming grasses and cheerful music. But something is unique to this park: it swallows the masses entirely. One does not have the image of a place full to the brim, unlike the Grunewald in Berlin which is only a vast feeding table, or in Vienna, at the Prater, when at the hour of returning home, it's like watching the flood of an army of people, veiled in its columns of dust, an image worthy of the Old Testament. In some way Hyde Park breaks up, shatters these masses. I felt it distinctly during the great workers' demonstration. In the streets a procession without end, a fluttering multitude of flags, a smoke of red light, a relentless marching, unceasing flux. But then in the park, all dissolved into one circle, and all around spread the flat terrain, which knew nothing of this and within whose enclosure flocks of lambs grazed freely. But that is what is so singular about this park: its complexity. Different areas are completely foreign one to another. Even the great 'Rotten Row', with its numerous bends, is not, unlike our avenue at the Prater, an elegant and precise line of chalk traced clearly across the green Never can one be said to have mastered Hyde Park – never, nor London itself. And it's not like Paris, where one can claim to have already seen all, by descending the butte of Montmartre from the Sacré Coeur, to the Grands Boulevards by way of the Boulevard de L'Opéra and over the Seine to the Panthéon or the Luxembourg. Never does one grasp the essence in one go, neither in London nor in Hyde Park. Little by little one must become accustomed to the dimensions and the remote abundance, as Gulliver in the land of the giants did the cumbersome large people. He gives too much to all and too little to each.

Or more precisely: the truth is that Hyde Park gives nothing, one must bring everything to it. It is not a park where dreams are awoken and in the bushes, unforgettable memories await one, as would mysterious princesses. To my knowledge, no poet has sung of it, doubtless because despite its riches, it has never offered anything to any of them. It's not like those little parks inside which each hour is inscribed for eternity in the book of memory: not like the pretty parc Monceau which the Parisians willingly grant the name '*parc des amoureux*', where the white statues of the poets give off a lustre, in such an appealing way, to the depths of a well-tended nature, not like the little giardiano Giusti in Verona, where the black cypresses, like sombre thoughts, seize the soul, not like that bright little garden of the popes up above the fortress in Avignon where wild swans quiver on a blue lake and one has an unforgettable view of the Provençal landscape. Hyde Park offers no memory, unlike that splendid elm-walk leading to the Alhambra, nor exotic dreams like those in the royal gardens of Seville, or in Schönbrunn during a sunny day in September when a golden leafage is spread upon the paths, reminding one that there can be gentle joy even at the threshold of death. No – Hyde Park does not inspire dream, it inspires life, sport, elegance, liberty of movement. If it were reserved for gentle, half-dozing reveries without possessing a useful function, they would long ago have studded it with houses, laced it with roads, poured noise into it. Here one only loves the dream that will quickly be a reality. And England's true dream does not bear the name 'Hyde Park', but still remains, Italy.

– 1906

Antwerp

Again and again one finds the name of this town in the letters and orders of Napoleon. During the Spanish campaign, in the depths of the struggle for Madrid, in Rome, in Germany, in Russia, on the Ebro, on the Moscow River, on the Danube, as much in the midst of the bloodiest battles as in his palaces of Fontainebleau and St-Cloud, he ponders this his most cherished creation with worried concern. He orders his generals to seize workers from the construction yards of Brest and Toulon, he commands his managers to stockpile arms and to construct warehouses. An entire fleet must be readied here within two years – far too prolonged a period for his impatience – and the forests of Germany will supply the masts and beams. Two basins he has dug and redoubts on every side, as impregnable as Gibraltar this fortress must be, a fortress of defence from both land and sea. He takes advantage of the first respite between the campaigns against Austria and Spain to visit his work, and makes his entrance in April 1810 – *la joyeuse entrée* – with all the pomp of an eastern ruler. In a flagship he is drawn down Rupel, the canal, from Brussels to Antwerp; with hundreds of artillery pieces the new armada thunders a welcome, not since Charles V has Antwerp seen such an entrance, which Mackart had glorified in his most famous painting. Before his gaze, ships are being launched, he inspects the forts and shipyards. Above him toll the bells of century-old towers, and the burghers of Antwerp, beholden to his genius for new riches and for this scarcely hoped-for renewal of activity, prostrate themselves before him like a god.

With the quick insight of his gaze, which like a falcon on the battlefield knew how to identify the enemy's vulnerable flank, Napoleon had soon recognised the vital importance of this northern port. His fleet had been smashed by the English at

Trafalgar. Now he blocked them from the sea as they had blocked him from the continent. Nowhere had he got the better of them, his most dangerous enemies. He had looked to sever their vital nerve in Egypt and Gibraltar, twice the weapon had slipped from his grasp. Now he made of this town a formidable offensive weapon. Near the English in case of attack, yet organically linked to the French-speaking region, this excellent port made the ideal nest for a fleet poised to launch a sudden assault and to fall rapidly back, a nest perfect too for brooding more ships. There, the Scheldt in all its broadness spreads into the sea, but before it lies the isle of Walcheren which, flanked on right and left by heavy batteries, such as Charybdis and Scylla,[9] threatens any potential invader. The Flemish hinterland and its fields radiant with grain, its flocks satisfyingly grazing the salty grasses dismiss all dangers of famine, and the sea wall, easy to breach in times of siege, can quickly transform the town into an armoured island. It was at this point and nowhere else that Napoleon would turn the world of the English upside down, and with all the fiery will of his temperament, in ten years he reinforces the merchant city neglected by the Austrian government, making of it a formidable fortress that effectively repels any English attack, and which, even during the empire's collapse, remains the only foreign port in French hands until the moment peace is signed. Like an armoured fist the city is stretched towards the mortal foe, towards England, and will fall only when Europe and its forces strike at the very heart of France, in Paris.

But the love of Napoleon for Antwerp is not only explained by sober knowledge of strategy, for the romantic in him, in his constant striving to establish a relation between his own genius and those of the past, looked to associate his name in some lasting way with the town. Venice, Rome, Moscow, Constantinople, all these cities, once mistresses of the world empire, exercised a pull on a spirit accustomed to departing the rational for the supernatural, and which is often drawn also towards super-stition, a peculiar fascination and in most cases a fatal one. Antwerp seduced him above all with its aura of invincibility, for no siege since the time of the Romans was at that time as famous as that of the Flemish town of which Schiller gave us a classical description, with truly dramatic effect in its twists and turns of plot.[10] (One can only cordially recommend all to reread it today, for by way of chance, present circumstances happily lead us to this great work.) He, the upstart, is galvanised by the memory of Charles V, ruler of the two worlds, who paraded his army here, and secretly his will wishes to see the prestige of the illustrious city revived thanks to his name. With his enormous vital force he breathed new life into a casual backwards-looking town, rekind-ling in her the extinguished flame of riches and power; however, the meteor-like speed of his own rise and decline meant he saw only the beginning of this glorious renewal, not its conclusion.

An isolated monument still bears witness today to this ancient world hegemony of Antwerp: the cathedral, whose vault domin-ates the town and port, transporting one to the grandiloquent days of Charles V and his ancestors. In that time the decline of Bruges and Ghent began, their ports silted up with sand and with the ports the riches ebbed away. Antwerp on the other hand, situated beside the running waves of the Scheldt, prospered until it acquired an almost tropical opulence. Rubens, the master, in some way a symbol of its magnificence, brought his effusive joy for colour into the grey world of the north, the barbarous sen-suality of his Hellenism. What Venice is for the south, Antwerp becomes for the north. From all parts of the world the rare merchandise comes: essences and fabrics, wood and stones; the taste for the luxurious incites the search for the strange, and the painters – Rubens in the north, like Titian and Tintoretto in the south – feast on the colours, as their countrymen on mater-ial possessions. Whilst in London and Amsterdam – cities of

Protestant sobriety – and in the virtuous towns of the Hanse,[11] they are content to hoard their gains, in Antwerp it just flows, glittering like jewellery on women, gathered in collections of curiosities and paintings, and with Master Plantin takes the form of precious books.[12] The 'New Carthage', as they proudly refer to their native town, does not aspire like Venice to world hegemony and glory, but applies itself with zeal to its commerce and draws profit from its earnings: here they enjoy living, and thus the blade of the Inquisition falls upon them.

All that makes for the grandeur of Antwerp dates from this period, from the time of Rubens, and also from our current epoch. Towns, even those of today, are always built in superimposed layers, as revealed by the dissection of Troy, a discovery of Schliemann. Ceaselessly they bury their own past, but the most powerful aspect of each epoch remains and bridges intact, so to speak, each renewal. Antwerp was obliged to recreate once more under a different form its one-time splendour and opulence. In the past, after the devastation wrought by the Spanish and the indolence of the Austrian regime, all that remained to her was that vital artery of her life, the Scheldt, which today as a century ago brings in ships and sends them back into the distance, and her sheer sword of God: the cathedral, the splendid pommel with delicate blade thrust towards the heavens. Some churches still survive, the town hall of Cornelius de Vriendt,[13] the Steen; but for a long time now, imposing arteries have exploded the labyrinth of low wooden houses. The new prosperity demands space around it and admiration. Proud and peaceable, the residences of rich merchants stand on the Meir, in the self-assurance of their splendour; inaccessible, lit solely by the green of the gardens are the villas on the banks of the Scheldt. Antwerp has no other style than opulence. Theatres and exhibitions bear testament to this: the taste for art is not extinguished in the home town of Pierre Paul Rubens, and in the outlying districts frequented by sailors a glance through a window often recalls the earthy scenes of a Jan Steen or a Terborch.[14] But these are only shades and reflections of the past: long has the old Flemish sensuality been lost to cosmopolitanism. Antwerp is not Brussels or Liège, where one always feels, despite the expanse of space, the narrowness and timidity of a provincial town: here the wind of the world blows, coming off the open sea. There is nothing static in the air here. In life, in the streets, in the interminable movements of the crowd, in the permanent whirlpool of the Bourse – giant funnel, which holds all activity in a furious cacophony – one perceives an intention that goes beyond the affairs of the day and the hour. Only Hamburg perhaps evokes America as forcefully as commercial Antwerp does, and that's why it cannot be by chance that one hears so much German spoken in the streets. Infiltrating through the subterranean channels of commerce, well before crossing the frontier itself, the corporation of German businessmen has taken possession of the Emporium. They have conquered whole streets, and their signs flock as far as the port, which they encircle with their docks and their offices.

Just there, on the banks of the Scheldt, one senses Antwerp's grandeur. An hour from here, in the green open spaces, towards Bornhem and St Amands, in the charming little villages, it's still a beautiful peaceful river that one sees, reflecting white clouds, with loaded flower boats and low ferries, a meadow between meadows almost, softly shifting and blue. And suddenly, barely has it transformed itself into the bay sheltering the port before it is blanketed by a forest of masts, a thousand different roars and cries stir into its tide, night and day it knows no rest; the great American steamers come in close, the small motorboats whirr amongst them, it's like watching vast swarms of bees enter and leave the honeycomb of the docks. There, they deposit from their wings the precious nectar, the goods. The cranes moan with pleasure when their fingers plunge into ships and exhume from

43

the darkness objects of value drawn from distant lands. Now and then the wharves ring out with signals, great clocks hammer out an exhortation to the emigrants to exchange a last greeting, all languages of the earth resound together here. And at once you understand the sense of this town, too great for this small country: for it must be at the service of all Europe, of an entire continent. But in vain has it attracted to itself the world hegemony of former times, only for itself and its own profit and not for the nation, not for a people. It's true, the 'New Carthage', the port of brokers and businessmen, isn't like Marseilles, the southern gateway of an empire, nor like Hamburg, the universal will of a people. Homeless for centuries, sometimes under the governance of Spain, sometimes the Netherlands, then the Austrians and the French, long has Antwerp been cosmopolitan, the booty of the strongest and the most competent, who won it thanks to the superiority of their trading power or by military force. Always it has grown towards others: Charles V, Napoleon, always the strongest of the hour. For the last time, the old town lives today the tragedy of a resistance against the inevitable, and the words of Schiller in the introduction to his celebrated account of the siege of Antwerp now apply to Germany. 'It's a spectacle worthy of interest to observe the inventive spirit of men contending with a powerful element, and to see seemingly insurmountable difficulties defeated by shrewdness, determination and an iron will.'

– 1914

Requiem for a Hotel

Surely I would not permit myself – oh surely not – to raise an objection, I a foreigner, against the decision of the City of Zurich to acquire the very old and famous Hotel Schwert and transform it into a tax office, but it has to be said, it's a genuine shame. For it was the bearer of a tradition unrivalled in Switzerland or almost anywhere else in Europe; a continuity is obliterated that evolved across centuries, from the town's very first stirrings, a glorious constancy across time destroyed forever. With the vanishing of residences of this kind, a significant portion of the town's soul also vanishes and what one generation sees painlessly depart, a few years later will prove a grievous loss to the next. I still remember the day in Vienna when workmen arrived with their shovels and began to demolish the house on Schwarzspanierstrasse where Beethoven died. At that time, it barely merited attention, yet today all covertly clench their fists in passing before the formless block of flats that stands in its place. If it were possible to redeem it, one would now find millions to perform the task – 'For only loss reveals true value.'

As for the old Hotel Schwert, it remains where it is. No stone will be displaced beyond another. And yet something has been stripped forever: its character. Its character and its renown: it was the city's oldest inn, having welcomed countless important men for seven centuries, and thus a chain that could have continued across the ages is being severed. It would have become each day more venerable, each year more famous, and one would have loved it more for this invisible phenomenon, for this magical aura formed of strangeness and piety that emanated from its very being; one would have loved it as one loves those few ancient hotels of Europe, the Elephant in Weimar, the Kaiserkrone in Bolzano, the Voltaire in Paris, to name only a few that make up our universal heritage. But not of value to everyone of course.

For many, good central heating and American-style comfort count for more than memories, but without resorting to sentimentalism, anyone sensitive to history experienced the presence of its strong and distinguished tradition. Who had not frequented these rooms during the seven centuries of their existence? Kaisers and kings, electors and margraves; but what is even more important is to remember that Mozart stayed here, on his way from Paris; Goethe resided for a long period, and certain of his most important works had in these very rooms their earthly homeland. Casanova lived his enchanted affair here, which one can read about in his memoirs. Cagliostro lived here under an assumed name; Fichte was the tutor of the hotelier; Madame de Staël, accompanied by August William Schlegel, stopped off here en route to Vienna. Who was here, who was not here? So clearly understood was it that the foreigner would stay at the Schwert that the coachmen, without bothering to ask questions, would drive those recently arrived in Zurich through narrow streets as far as the Limmat bridge. This place represented the city's unwritten register of travellers for seven centuries. Every person of note had stayed there.

In the nineteenth century, it is true, when the stagecoaches gave way to the railway and inns to hotels, this signalled a decline for the ancestral house. Then the Baur au Lac, which for some decades had been recognised as the foremost hotel of prestige in Europe, stole its reputation. Hemmed in between the road and the river, the old Hotel Schwert could not expand, transform its narrow entrance into a magnificent foyer – it was left behind. But it's only because it remained identical to itself, refusing to follow modern times in their frantic search for novelties more luxurious with each passing year, that it acquired a charm of a different kind, the charm of antiquity. People cherished it in the manner of an old piece of furniture, of a Folio book dating from their ancestors; they cherished it with the modest emotion that faded objects arouse in us, which cannot be fully explained by reasoning. How many times, in some old street, before an old chateau, is one prey to this mysterious desire, 'Here is where I would like to live' – perhaps simply because of the sense of futility in such a wish. Perhaps because of the deeply embodied heritage that runs through our veins, and unbeknownst to us, we feel a love for these places as if we had always lived in them. The Hotel Schwert amply fulfilled this habitual unrealisable yearning. So it was that during the war years, drawn one by the other, and without conferring, virtually all foreign artists stayed at the Hotel Schwert. In the same way as all true glories, this one was not by any means indebted to publicity; it rested upon words transmitted with love by word of mouth. If its celebrity had been brashly flaunted, as was the case for the Ratskeller of Bremen or Torggelstube of Bolzano, if everywhere had been announced, 'Here resided Goethe, Mozart, Kaiser Joseph,' etc., one would have felt unease at the idea of lodging in a house of curiosities (rather like in Paris when one flees the Hotel '*Aux grands hommes*'). But here there was a tacit agreement, a literary Freemasonry.

Of course: one did not stay in this now-deceased hotel simply because of such a magical aura, of course not! One chose it because, in its particular way, it was both beautiful and welcoming. According to an ancestral tradition belonging to inns, the office was managed not by a head of reception, but by the owner in person. It was always touching to observe the affable white-haired Herr Jölden, with his little cap on, moving from table to table; his wife, his daughter, his son actively working together, so one avoided experiencing the uncomfortable feeling of strangeness. The place was hardly luxurious, the old house put up a mysterious resistance to all technical innovations, as if tradition were defending itself against modernity. The lift was content to remain jammed, the central heating emitted more a death rattle than any heat and the telephone remained a reluctant foreign body to these walls of a bygone time. But how marvellous the bright dining room, entered through heavy and magnificent wooden doors: one felt as if upon the glass-covered deck of a great steamer, before one, behind one, water, the Limmat, and at a distance the lake and the fine contours of the mountains. On the bridge of vegetables, the vibrant colours of flowers shone out, the towers of the cathedral hailed you, instinctively you felt at the heart of the city. For the foreigner who wants to discern the culture of a certain place, it is essential either in some way to sense the flavour of the land from the nucleus of its settlement, or to encompass the whole by looking from the outside, from a position of height. Here the two conditions were united: there were several rooms on the top floor where one found oneself right in the middle of the city of Zurich and at the same time above it, where one could see it rise from its centre and lose itself in the distances towards the hills and lake. Sometimes, one almost had the impression that the whole town had been constructed and arranged around this single house, so judicious was the positioning of this inn at the heart of the landscape.

One knew then, as in our time, as always and everywhere, both light and dark hours. And one had already silently looked forward to returning years later, in times of peace, and by means of memory, to savour in a more profound and agreeable way that epoch now passed. One said to oneself, 'You will always come back to stay here,' and the feeling rooted itself in every one of us that this house so anterior to us would survive us all, that we were but a name in the centuries-old register formed of wood and stone. But there, war does not care for predetermination; it also destroys in fury that which is immaterial, the hopes and expectations. With steel tread it tramples traditions, and as it has deprived Berlin of its only truly handsome large hotel built before the epoch of the nouveau riche, the Kaiserhof, and in Frankfurt the Schwan, where peace was signed between France and Germany, it deprived Zurich of its oldest inn. One will return and, in place of the friendly invitation, one will find a less pleasant inscription: 'Tax Office' – a building whose threshold even a better citizen than I crosses with reluctance. In the room where the young Mozart, symbol of life's musical weightlessness, resided, folds of dossiers will be consulted. In Goethe's lodgings, an austere commissioner will be exercising his functions. In the room where once Casanova, disguised as a waiter, showed an excessive consideration to beautiful ladies, the citizens will be submitted to a rigorous inquisition. Only the spirit of Cagliostro, the great alchemist, will remain alive, and his art of emptying and filling purses will be practised by means of a tedious game of figures and not by cheerful deception. Perhaps it will bring much money back to the city of Zurich, this building destined to apply the gentle pressure of a wider community on the individual; however, all the money in the world cannot compensate for what has been lost: a part of the city's soul, a precious fragment of tradition. But maybe we, the foreigners, more powerfully sense the magic at work with these transforming materials, we, without right to issue protest but who have no intention of stifling our regret, and express it by this one modest word, that in truth is a sigh, the word: 'shame'.

– 1918

Return to Italy

For us who have known the European world as a living entity, where frontiers blurred into one another in a scarcely perceptible way, to see again another country has for a long time, perhaps forever, led to a constant comparison of past and present. Everywhere we look, as in our own country, at the visible manifestations of what once was; our present impressions are unwearyingly drawn to rediscover those of former times; we are no longer just looking, we are recalling ourselves as we were then and in recalling ourselves we realise the change, the metamorphosis that each of us has personally undergone. In the same way as we are constantly making conversions, in spite of ourselves, noting the collapse and fluctuations in monetary value of each foreign item, so we measure the importance of the transformation in our inner tension. All of our generation who lived to see this transition will perhaps never be able to confront the world again with the full freedom of their objective gaze; it has become our destiny then to subject our sensations to comparison and reminiscence, with the clearer shadow of the past upon the darkened image, and to associate each impression directly transmitted to our eyes with that experienced previously.

Thus, during those first hours in Italy, impelled by an inner curiosity – and I know that thousands of men in our closed-in country will do the same – you ask yourself what exactly has changed here during those years? Reassured, in deep joy, with an ever more certain knowledge one may reply: not much. And above all, nothing of great significance. Nature senses the most extreme crises of humanity as having about the same impact as the arrows of the dwarves of Brobdingnag on Gulliver: they leave little more than a pinprick. For nature, the age of a people only counts for an hour, war barely a second. The essential lives on here as in the past, but perhaps everyone feels it with more intensity for having been deprived of it for so long: intact, the white lace of Milan Cathedral quivers, reaching towards the sky; the palaces of Genoa are lined up in their ancient splendour; the most marvellous stairway in the world descends to the foaming sea below. Tuscany blooms its eternal springtime across time and Venice dreams its colourful dream. Even there where the war has engraved a few slight scars, at bullet-ridden Riva, in the mountain fortresses, and also with the people, one already finds no trace of hostility, or at least of hate. The people are just as in former times, filled with that joyful liveliness that seems merely to make a game of work: one notices nothing of that acrimony that, at home, makes existence so unbearable; right to the heart of the social struggles, which like a volcano overwhelm the country, one finds a certain relish for the fight, an honest lively courage. Never have I felt so powerfully the vitality of Italy and its indestructible energy in spite of all the crises that now traverse it. (And these are even more evident when you enter from Austria, where a growth of tension in the intellectual sphere is equally noticed everywhere.)

Italy has not changed, nor the Italians. The few external manifestations (which are fundamentally insignificant), an increase in the cost of living, the as-yet only partially resolved difficulties of supply, felt as consequences of war, are absolutely a European characteristic rather than a national one. And yet you discern in the image of the big cities a distinct transformation. What has changed are the travellers, foreigners who to a greater extent than one imagined influenced the way one thinks of the physiognomy of the most visited towns in Italy. Above all it seems there are less of them. To travel abroad today has become what it always was, and only ceased to be a decade or two before the war because of improvements in comfort and the fall of prices: an effort, something laborious and in material terms almost a luxury. Thus all countries are now more national than they were before, and so Italy too is more Italian than it was before; elegance no longer belongs to foreigners, but to its native women – and here too the immeasurable increase in levels of luxury due to the *Pesce cane* (the name given to war profiteers) is visible everywhere. And then even in the type of tourist a most radical mutation has taken place. There too, the order now adheres to the official list of values: in the first rank the English and the neutral countries, the Swiss, the Scandinavians, the Dutch. On the other hand the Austrians, the Hungarians are swept away and the Germans, formerly the largest contingent of travellers to Italy, are reduced to a modest number.

Only he who knew Italy in the years before the war could assess changes in the external appearance of Italian towns following this ostracisation of the German element, and he will therefore see it as a fortunate transformation for both Germany and Italy. For travel to Italy had become a German fashion, and more and more an invasion that washed ashore en masse the whole family of the provincial petit bourgeois – as one encounters it in Sternheim and Heinrich Mann – so in the end one no longer tasted the aroma of Italy, but only that world that is felt as highly antipathetic to the cultivated German. They had transformed St Mark's square into a feeding area for pigeons, Capri into a room for Skat,[21] Rimini and the Lido into an Ischl by the sea. Between the palaces nest the Gambrinus halls,[22] and the loden coat threatens to become the new national costume. This rowdy boisterous Germany – to the delight not only of the Italians – has vanished from the towns, and the Germans one sees now are the more agreeable element; to put it in literary terms, the Thomas Mann German, the quiet, cultivated one described with so much love by the author, in opposition to the Heinrich Mann German, the petit bourgeois stigmatised with so much ironical hatred by his brother. The new component of the populace, the black marketer element, still does not venture to leave the country; they are too uncertain in manner, too unsound in their language skills, and visibly deprived of their preferred pleasure: to be envied for their recent fortunes. For they sense quickly, unlike the Americans, the illusory nature of their millions of crowns, and compared to real works of art they well see that their Biedermeyer antiquities and Marie-Theresien furniture, purchased at too high a cost, appear poor substitutes. The traveller to a foreign country has become what he once was, though in the last years only when travelling overseas: representative of the more elevated, intellectual circles of his nation, and not an average man, the working mass, whom by way of their herd instinct are always repellent.

One rejoices then for these two nations of the chosen elite and one would be still more happy if, among that so raucous mass that formerly visited Italy, one did not miss a valuable type in an altogether different sense: the young person, the artist, the painter, the poet, who, coming here not to follow fashion or annoy their neighbours in some small provincial town by sending postcards, became conscious in these places for the first time, in a more liberated intellectual climate, that the grandeur of the past went hand in hand with a new world that knows no national boundaries. I see us again, we the young of all nations, Germans, Scandinavians, English, Italians, poets, art historians, painters, musicians, those from the most diverse classes, conditions and peoples, joined in the act of happily wandering across Florence and Rome, galvanising each other through our passion and enthusiasm. Over the course of these days (as over the course of quite a few others in Paris), our generation learnt a kind of close camaraderie that life within the narrow confines of the home country never permits one to know; inalienable years and hours for each were these days and nights in Italy, so much so that just to hear the word Italy, joyous youth resounds in all of us. These young people, I come across them no more: the door of Italy is closed to them because of the precarious nature of existence, the image of Italy misses their joy so much, as the joy of Italy is missed by them. It is them I cannot desist from evoking here, these young people of our world, the isolated and excluded, that youth for which a book is now a precious object, a theatre seat a sacrifice, a journey an impossibility; those who are condemned to live in the claustrophobic atmosphere of today's Austria, to have their spirit poisoned by it. And if I had to speak to young people, my first objective would be to exhort them to deploy all efforts to save for themselves the possibility of retaining some view on the world and maintaining a freedom of the spirit. This is still possible for the resolute individual to achieve, and the young man who rightly renounces daily sending up thirty to sixty crowns in cigarette smoke can all the same permit himself one week or one month a year in this country and in doing so he will infinitely enrich his entire existence. One does not owe one's learning to academies, to paintings, to museums, that is for certain, but it's true also that there is no real intellectual activity without an expansive field of vision, without capacity for comparison. And, among the neighbouring countries of our dismembered country, Italy with the cheerful luminosity of her sky remains the potent idea of Europe, the beautiful vision of a necessary, new art, gratefully linked to antiquity, the best path to eternity. She is still our Arcadia, the mystical image of a submerged pure sphere, eternally new as on the first day, and a source of happiness each time one discovers her.

– 1921

The Cathedral of Chartres

Never was Paris so powerful, so dazzling as this year, nor so
radiant with inner energy, resplendent in abundant light: another
more vehement rhythm shakes the streets and those who until
then knew the gentle breathing of this beloved town, feel amaze-
ment and almost a horror to find how hot, how passionate, and
verging on the febrile it has now become. Something of New
York, the tempo of the American metropolis permeates the
avenues: a white and blinding light pours over streets swarm-
ing with bodies, from roof to roof luminous placards leap and
the houses shake right up to their ridge tiles with the rumble of
automobiles. The colours, the stones, the squares, all glows and
flickers and burns with this new velocity, down in the thundering
cavern of the Metro every nerve of this dazzling town vibrates
and every fibre of one's body unconsciously trembles along with
it. One feels as though hounded onwards, propelled as if from
a gun, borne on this dizzying intoxication that stuns and delights
but at the same time leaves one so weary. Pleasure glutted is this
tempo, a phantasmagoria of glances, powerful excitement – but
then time and again comes that moment when a man tells himself 'enough!' One would like to be calm for a while, to rest,
to stroll the old lanes of the left bank, on the Boul'Mich,[23] so
cherished in youth. But the old lanes are no longer the place for
a relaxing promenade: as if fired like projectiles from the barrel
of a cannon, one automobile after another is shot relentlessly out
of their narrow throats. And on the Boul'Mich the banks (as
everywhere) have replaced the cafés – the youth, the students
have been pushed out to the suburbs, to Montparnasse. Nowhere is it possible to find a half hour's peace from one morning
to the next in this swollen feverish city. Even as far as St-Cloud
and Sèvres her nerves still twitch with restless affliction. Nowhere, nowhere any longer '*la douce France*', nowhere one can

go, come evening, to admire the silvery light over the Seine, nowhere any longer the old Paris; the gentle sensual warm town has turned muscular and beats time like a frantic labourer – her lustre hisses upwards like the flickering play of a rocket. One must go far behind her English and American face to discover France, to sense the France of old, to find pleasure in experiencing this Paris that now explodes into a thousand flying sparks. And suddenly, longing for an hour of repose, I remember that among the great cathedrals, Chartres is the only one I have not seen; an hour and a half's journey from here, and I know already in advance: between it and Paris lie a thousand years – and there the pendulum of time keeps an altogether more easeful rhythm.

Strange, the express train rattling in flight past the telegraph poles seems something of a relief already after the shimmer-play of Paris. One leans against the window and looks out at the open countryside: the view seems familiar, for one has that feeling of knowing, through the canvases of the Impressionists, every tree, every canal, every pool. How often have Monet, Pissarro, Renoir, Sisley painted them all, the little gardens in the moist sheen of spring's awakening, the shy birches, the shining grasses, this land so opulent yet flat, this fulsome and yet rather monotone land around Paris? Never a proper forest, never a hill, never even from the distance a real mountain; only meadows, houses and water, ardently cultivated and fully harnessed. Already the vision wearies, all around there is nothing to hold the eye; but suddenly, as the train begins to slow, something powerful stands erect in this low-lying landscape, overwhelmingly powerful even, a huge and commanding structure. 'Like a kneeling giant who raises his arms over the flat plains towards God,' was how Paul Claudel[24] began one of his incantations on the French cathedral. And of a sudden these lines came back to me with the violent onset of a truth: in fact, like a stranger, like a mighty colossus, a cathedral raises its heavy and massive bulk above the flat expanse of a provincial town, and raised in a gesture of eternal prayer, the two towers above it reach out to the heavens. How senseless it seems for such a colossal edifice to shoot up here, in the middle of an empty landscape, in the middle of a low-lying unremarkable town, but it is precisely that which gives the impression of such unforgettable magnificence. In Paris one finds it understandable that in the ceaseless turbulence of the streets, Notre Dame like a huge well gathers into herself the faith of millions of beings, and one can scarcely imagine Vienna or Cologne without their stone spires, to which the tangle of houses surges up, so to speak; but here the dimension comes as a shock, the scale as an experience.

Who constructed it then, this mighty cathedral in the void of the landscape, reigning over that modest and ordinary town? The names of the builders are forgotten, and even if they were known one would learn little from them. For one person or isolated individuals cannot create such marvels, which require whole centuries in order to exist properly, and for their immortality to ripen fully. The real builders here were named Faith and Patience: the faith of thousands of lost names, forgotten people, and the patience of thousands upon thousands of solitary workmen. In vain, one scrutinises the lines, the plans. One receives no response to the inevitable question: from where in olden times did these individuals draw the courage to erect such a giant cathedral, in the vacancy of nature, barely attached to an inappreciable town? Was it not the aim, as in Paris, powerful sister, to surpass the ambition of those who raised the churches of Italy, the cathedrals of Germany, the belfries of Belgium, each one mightier than those that went before? Or perhaps, a long time before, here where one sees barely a hillock rise above the meadows, a man had lived who, having noticed mountains and towering rocks through the course of distant travels, revealed to others his desire to build something to such a height that one might from any angle watch eagle-like from horizon to horizon. In any case, they set out to build a mountain of stone, a citadel of God powerfully anchored against the rush of time, and they worked without respite until its completion. Each generation picked up from the last and thus grew this colossal vault with its towers ascending to the glinting pinnacle, to the airy home of the bells.

But once this vault of rock was built, doubtless they were seized by dread, these people of a fair and sunlit land, for the interior must have been dark and cold as a cave. The tremendous nature of this vaulted heap of stone surely breathed gloom and a secret terror: in answer they installed coloured panes in the caverns of the windows to lessen the burden of that grey light, allowing the sun to filter through all their colours, and so here too the myriad colourations of life made one sense even in this darkness a certain ecstatic bliss. These stained glass windows of Chartres are of a splendour without rival. Less crowded than those of St-Chapelle in Paris (which are in fact only glittering glass intersected by narrow bands of stone), they divide the rigid walls into blue ovals, into glowing rosettes infinitely multiform: just as in the grotto of Capri, arriving from an invisible distance, a light of violet and cobalt blue magically radiates in an incredible binding and scattering about the space, which now dissolves into an indescribable twilight. Each of these colours is full and bright, each has a purity and a depth only possessed on this variegated earth by the flowers of the Alps; the gentian, the hellebore, the edelweiss are all of a glowing intensity that our modern chemistry and thundering factories are no longer capable of fusing with liquid glass. Although in the midst of coolness and lofty height, one feels as if on fire, in a solitary rapture of gazing.

However, for those nameless ones there was still insufficient life in that towering building. Certainly the rock was flower-bedecked and radiant; it had become nature, landscape. But it still lacked the true life – man, in all his forms – and the swarms of animals. So they mounted portraits, figures in stone all over to revive the rigidity of the rock: incalculable is the number of this flock. Before the portals, severe-looking guardians, angels and patriarchs stand in relief from the pillars in the unsparing, narrow gothic style, and from niches appear the jagged wings of bat creatures, while from the tower's summit the gargoyles lean out their gaping mouths. These figures fill the vaults with their whirling mass, they are like an ever-moving story and around the altar they form a sculptural representation of the holy legend. The Annunciation, the Nativity and the Resurrection, the holy festivals of the year, the Golden Legend, the Prodigal Son and the Good Samaritan: one sees it all here breathing in stone, in the refined glow of the windows, and these figures are so abundant no one can possibly count them all. There must be thousands or tens of thousands – like thickets and under-growth, the human figures force their way between the rising trunks of the pillars, straining to reach up into the vault. All styles, all forms are assembled, and the wall around the altar initiated by Jean de Beauce in the fourteenth century and real-ised only in the eighteenth reflects every variety of sculpture: one has in just a few minutes traversed whole centuries in the history of art. And one knows one cannot see it all, since en-tire generations of stonemasons and sculptors have devised this earthly army assembled here in eternal praise to God.

But this immeasurable flock that covers the pillars, the crypt, the vault and the walls to be properly sensed needs the living men of today. It's Sunday and the inhabitants of the town are filling the cathedral: well, these are merely words, for in fact they do not fill it at all. They occupy only a few benches, here and there they cluster together before an image; but how feeble and miserable is this handful of individuals against the infinite number of figures in stone, how minuscule the web of the faithful within the immensity of the cathedral. For this church had room for an entire generation and that is its heroic lesson, eternally big enough for all earthly aspirations, eternally able to exceed all possibilities and now forever a symbol of infinity. They simply wished to immortalise their faith, those who raised this cathedral in the heart of this flat country, forging in stone to preserve their pious will beyond their own time. Reverent, one senses here 'the spirit of the gothic', that century of faith and patience, a century never to return. For never again will such works arise in our epoch, which measures time in a different way and lives at an altogether different pace: man will build no more cathedrals.

Man will build no more cathedrals: that's the impression of penury one experiences when rejoining our world having taken leave of this long-standing monument. Our plans demand accomplishment at speed, our rhythm of life becomes ever more frantic, and there is no single work that lasts beyond a generation and none even that reaches beyond a single life. We who thanks to a spark are capable of communicating with another continent in a second, we no longer know how to articulate our being across the slowness of stones, the infinitude of years. Our miracles are manageable and intellectual, our dreams more compact. Now the soul takes leave of the huge rising form of something that has become alien to it, like the Pyramids or the Parthenon; we have lost our capacity for the eternal, which the world itself has gained, and our capacity to incarnate the spirit of a whole people or the genius of a time in a *single* work. So then, it's over: men will build no more cathedrals.

And yet, as the return train made its way through the darkening evening landscape, before the sight itself, the presentiment of Paris loomed: the giant city, a glowing cupola atop a reddish vault on the horizon, rising up into an invisible sky. It's the circle of fire that is Paris; another cathedral stands there, night after night, without foundations or stones – and instead of Chartres' hundreds of thousands of stone blocks, hundreds of thousands of lights and electric flames. Indestructible, this glowing dome of light reigns above the seething nocturnal city, this union of count-less electrical energies and the fervently pulsing lives of millions forms the most impressive cathedral of our epoch. Maybe it has not emerged from the same faith as the ancient cathedrals, but one finds the same burning desire, the same immortal human energy. Radiant with celestial light and raised on high in the listening night, this new cathedral of Paris would perhaps have appeared to the builders of yesterday just as splendid, as mighty and divine as the works they left seem now to our eyes. Epochs have used different signs to engrave their face on the landscape of the earth, and nothing is more wonderful than in the space of an hour to read, to understand and to love (as much as they may seem strangers to each other) one sign *and* the other expressing their will to live.

– 1924

The Fair of Good Eating

God alone knows what curious fete I had stumbled upon when, returning from Marseilles, I stopped off at Dijon to visit at last her museum and its magnificent tombs of the dukes of Burgundy! Exiting the station, one is greeted by splendid pennants of all colours. There are thousands of little coloured flags, which in the clear light of day dance like tiny flames, while the music of jingling merry-go-rounds drifts from somewhere, and just at the moment when you ask yourself with some surprise in which saint's honour this festive garb might be worn, the answer shouts gaudily in front of you, inscribed on the banners stretched over the street: '*Foire Gastronomique*', or, as I prefer to translate it, 'The Fair of Good Eating'. Yes, such a thing exists in today's gloomy world, a thing that has taken place annually for five years in Dijon, the ancient Burgundy city that recalls Augsburg in the splendour of its private mansions; a fair for eating well, solemnly inaugurated by the minister and mayor, with speeches of great vigour and mediocre poems, but also, it seems, offering notable wines and fancy food. All the restaurants are obliged, on each day of the three week period, to prepare in competition with the rest several specific dishes, which like pieces of music on the festival programme are noted with care weeks in advance: a culinary calendar it would seem to me far more arduous to render into our beloved German language than, say, a poem of Paul Valéry or Mallarmé into German verse. On the streets they nibble on freshly baked waffles, before shops piled high with hundreds of thousands of those delectable – so they say – Burgundy snails, which disappear now at a greater speed with wine drawn from the vine around which they habitually climb. Cooks in their white chef's hats with ceremonious reddened faces are here more or less like officers are in Germany: objects of boundless admiration and uncontested masters of the situation. And since at the same time a *Foire aux Vins*, a wine trade fair, is taking place, you spot buyers of all nations tantalised by the many tastings, drawn through the streets, eyes a touch hazy but blinking cheerfully. They are somewhat loud, the bulky fellows, their faces having taken on a coppery sheen, but they are merry, jovial and contented; arranged like friendly catchflies in frockcoats, they are an agreeable part of the high-spirited picture.

Sincerely though, is it not heartening that there are still such innocent fairs – exuberant, without pretension, where the true essence of human nature is reflected – in a world, as I was saying, become so morose and yet in another sense so deafening? I myself know that this refined delicacy is an art destined for the pleasure of the body and thus a minor one – though the French have never ceased to regard good cuisine as an art – while I am far from comparing the high-spirited festive air of such a fair to, for example, that unforgettable pleasurable inward curve I experienced this year at the Handel festival in Leipzig. No, not to compare them but also not arrogantly to curl one's lip, when a people, when a town has the courage to be joyful and is carefree in proclaiming the more simple aspects of existence, and through a most tender love, a dogged passion, grants status to the less important. It is precisely then this carefree nature, this jovial gaiety for the small things that best expresses a well-defined trait of the French character barely known in Germany, for at home all eyes are too relentlessly fixed on Paris, which, sadly, is rapidly losing its Frenchness, and is a great cause for concern, becoming a cosmopolitan city with the way of life fitting to a cosmopolitan city. So it is to the provinces one must go if one wishes to understand the true meaning of France. Only there, in such Lilliputian festivals, in jubilant spirits, in vain futility, are exposed all peculiarities. That's what I see here in Dijon, at this fair, a rare spectacle these days: cheerfulness that is never raucous but comes from within, linked to that pleasure aroused by trifles, which must be created day after day, an uncommon occurrence that I thought had long since departed us to reside with the negroes. Perhaps I only made these observations in a moment of lucidity, still tainted by the pale, delicate wine offered alongside the sumptuous repast. But still, I saw and felt it all for a few hours. That is why I gladly include this fair of Dijon in the book of happy remembrances, *nel libro della mia memoria*.[25]

– 1925

To Travel or be 'Travelled'

Stations and ports, these are my passion. For hours I can stand there awaiting a fresh wave of travellers and goods noisily crashing in to cover the preceding one; I love the signs, those mysterious messages that reveal hour and journey, the shouts and sounds dull yet varied that establish themselves in an evocative ensemble of noise. Each station is different, each distils another distant land; every port, every ship brings a different cargo. They are the universe for our cities, the diversity in our daily life.

But now I see a new kind of station, and here in Paris for the first time; they stand in the middle of the street, without visible lobby or roof, there is nothing distinctive about them and yet they are the focus of an unrelenting tide of activity. This is the stop for automobiles destined for group travel, which one day perhaps will take over from the railcar: with them commences another kind of travel, travelling en masse, contractual travel, or being 'travelled'. Nine o'clock: the first detachment arrives from the boulevard, forty or fifty passengers, mostly American and English. An interpreter sporting a gaudy cap loads them into the vehicle, they are taken to Versailles, to the Loire chateaux, to Mont St Michel, even as far as Provence. For them a mathematical organisation has thought of everything in advance, prepared everything; they need search for nothing, figure out nothing; the car starts, they depart for a foreign city, lunch (included in the price) awaits them there, as does a bed for the night; museums, wonders are entirely at their disposition on arrival. Needless to hail a porter, to give a tip. For every gaze, a time has already been worked out in advance, the choice of journey is the fruit of long experience: how simple it all is! No need to worry about money, to prepare oneself, to read up from books, to go in search of lodgings – and behind these 'travelled' (I don't say 'travellers') stands, with colourful headwear, the guardian (because in a sense he is both a guard and a watchman), who mechanically explains to them each particularity. The sole movement required is to present oneself in a travel agency, to choose a destination, pay the required amount, purchase board and lodging of some description for fourteen days, as already your luggage precedes you and brownie functionaries have organised bed and breakfast at some unknown place – and thus, without lifting so much as a finger, thousands upon thousands of travellers arrive from England and America. Or the 'travelled', to be more precise.

I strive to imagine myself one day in the midst of such a group. The air of convenience surrounding the whole affair is undeniable. All the senses are marshalled for contemplation and pleasure: one's attention is not deflected by those Lilliputian worries, constant vexations over the search for shelter and lodgings, one is not obliged to consult railway timetables, one does not stumble into streets where one has no right to be, one does not put oneself in a position to be scoffed at, cheated, to stammer, knowing barely a few words of the foreign language – all the senses are primed exclusively to embrace novelty. Novelty, which, having passed through the sieve of several decades of experience, is reduced to mere curiosities: one only sees the bare essentials in this kind of group travel, company is always missed by those for whom pleasure is only effective when shared with others. Furthermore, it's good value, practical and above all easy – therefore the shape of things to come. One no longer travels, one is travelled.

And yet, is it not the most mysterious aspect of travel that will be lost in such a fortuitous arrangement? Since time immemorial, there has floated around the word 'travel' a whiff of danger and adventure, a breath of capricious chance and engrossing precariousness. When we travel, it's not only for the love of far-off lands; we also want to leave our own area behind, our domestic world so well regulated day to day; we are

66

drawn by the desire no longer to be at home and therefore no longer to be ourselves. We want to interrupt a life where we merely exist, in order to live more. So, to be 'travelled' in this manner, one must be content to pass before numerous novelties without actually experiencing them at all; all the strangeness, the distinctiveness of a country will utterly escape you as soon as you are led and your steps are no longer guided by the real god of travellers, chance. In fact, in their group automobile, these English and Americans remain in England and America, they never hear the native language, they have no consciousness of specificity and the customs of the people (for all friction is dismissed). They see things worth seeing, certainly, but twenty car loads daily see the same wonders, each sees what the other sees and the guide who is responsible for providing explanations always offers the same method of delivery. And no one feels it deep within, because it's a group; beneath a swell of words they approach those lofty values and most noble worlds, but they are never alone to observe, to spiritually absorb these marvels: what they take home is nothing but the righteous pride of having recorded with their eyes some church, or painting – more a sports record than the sense of any personal maturation and cultural enrichment.

Surely it is preferable then to accept the unpleasant, the difficult, the contrary aspects: for these make any travel experience worthy of the name; there is always a contradiction between comfort – an objective reached without sufferance – and the truthful lived experience. The vital component in life, all that we consider a gain is the fruit of an effort and of a resistance, all genuine intensification of our relationship with the world must in some way be united with the personal fibre of our being. That's why the ceaselessly perfected mechanism of travel seems to my mind more dangerous than beneficial for anyone who is not content to approach the unknown only at its exterior point, but seeks to reach into their soul for the truly powerful and vital image of a new landscape. There where we do not discover, or at least do not believe we will discover, where no concealed energy or fellow feeling drives us towards novelty, we miss a mysterious tension in the enjoyment, a link between the undisclosed and our incredulous gaze; and the less we allow experiences to reach us with casual ease, the more we will approach them in the true spirit of adventure and the more they shall be intimately grafted onto our being. The mountain railways are a marvellous accomplishment: in an hour, they can whisk you to the most awe-inspiring world; without fatigue and in considerable comfort, one may savour the panorama sloping away at one's feet. However, such a mechanical ascent deprives one of any physical stimulation, of that uncanny fizz of pride that accompanies the sense of conquest. They are deprived of this remarkable feeling, inherent to every true experience, all those who are travelled rather than travel, who, as they take out their wallet at the kiosk to pay for some tour, do not pay the higher price, the more valuable one: that of the inner will, the tension of its energy. The odd thing is it's precisely such a cost that will be reimbursed thereafter with the greatest extravagance. Indeed, only those impressions acquired through vexations, annoyances, mistakes, leave us with a clear and vibrant memory. We like nothing better than to recall the minor woes, the nuisances, the muddles and the mistakes brought about by travel, as when, approaching our twilight years, what we really hold dear to our hearts are the most foolhardy exploits of our youth. Our day-to-day lives follow the ever-more mechanical and stringently smooth ride upon the rails of a technologically seduced century, something we cannot prevent and perhaps don't wish to anyway, for this way we conserve our strength. But travel must be an extravagance, a sacrifice to the rules of chance, of daily life to the extraordinary; it must represent the most intimate and original form of our taste. That's why we must defend it against this new fashion for the bureaucratic, automated displacement en masse, the industry of travel.

Let us preserve this modest gap for adventure in a universe of acute regulation. Let us not hand ourselves over to these overly pragmatic agencies who shepherd us around like goods, let us continue to travel in the way our ancestors did, as we wish, towards the goal we ourselves have chosen. Only that way can we discover not only the exterior world but also that which lies within us.

– 1926

Ypres

A good number of years have passed since the day I found myself in this town now renowned for the tragedy that befell it. On leaving Bruges one faced two or three hours' journey in a rattling, coughing, branch line train, to arrive in the evening, a poor lone stranger obliged to go to considerable efforts to track down a hotel for the night. By nine o'clock the people were already abed and only a few estaminets could be glimpsed, the light of their oil lamps twinkling through half-closed shutters, the town square before the dark and deserted market place a pool in the shape of a quadrangle. Not a sound. Truth to tell, one would not have been at all surprised to see a medieval night watchman loom up from the shadows, sounding through the alleys the meistersingers'[26] nocturnal chant that the hour of sleep had come. Then, colossal but heaved out of the silence, the square mass of that magnificent edifice, the cloth hall. It was for this as much as the cathedral that I had come, a three hour journey by train across this slow and forgotten provincial backwater.

Presently the name of Ypres, the *ville martyre*, shouts from all the posters, from Lille to Ostend, from Ostend to Antwerp and far into Holland. Organised tours, excursions by automobile, individually tailored visits; it's a veritable bidding war. Every day some ten thousand people (perhaps more!) come to pass a few hours here: Ypres has become Belgium's star attraction, a dangerous competitor for Waterloo, a 'must-see' for all the tourists. Resistance, that is the initial sentiment one experiences at the idea of mixing with this herd of amateur battlefield enthusiasts. But a sense of responsibility moves us not to overlook any traces that bring to life in concrete terms the history of our epoch: for only in remaining so informed can we take on so terrifying a past and then be able to turn and face the future.

En route, then, for Ypres. But not in one of those buses with guides paid to reel off each day, according to an already determined itinerary, a varied programme composed of cemeteries, commemorative monuments, ruins and two hundred thousand dead. First a pleasant little detour to Nieuport. Wide convenient roads, a smooth ribbon of newly laid asphalt on which luxury cars with silent suspension thread from one coastal resort to another, probably without even noticing to left and right the vestiges of war, already little by little becoming obscured beneath a covering of sand. One must look keenly to make out a narrow channel of water zigzagging across a field, which was for four years a trench where battalions crouched. That round pond over there in which bluish clouds are reflected, where yellow-spotted cows with muzzles of a delicate pink hue peacefully graze, was originally a man-murdering crater made from the impact of a piece of heavy artillery.

Yes, one must surely have a keen eye to discern these memorials of the past (for time erases the traces in the shifting earth almost as quickly as in the amnesic minds of men). But as soon as one approaches Nieuport, the main old front line, the signs multiply in a disturbing fashion. More and more troglodyte caverns, then trees split right up to the foliage burnt by gas, erect, accusatory, their skeletal arms directed heavenwards. More and more abandoned and crushed corrugated roofs, the supports of dugouts; and a certain unease expresses itself deep inside one's being when one is faced with what may remain of the town of Nieuport, for years the target of artillery, daily pulverised and crushed to little more than ashes, over a period of forty horrific months. But no, with a sudden blow to the heart, one makes out in the distance, miraculously untouched, the silhouette of that small port town. As in times past, the elegant belfry traces itself in charcoal across the sky and the little houses with tiled roofs beam with their ruddy bricks and bright white panes. So to speak of total destruction was exaggerated. Now you see with your very own eyes: the town stands erect as before. Reassured, so to speak, you cross the Yser canal, which holds less water than all the blood shed by Europe's sons. Then you alight in the unchanged town, moving along the streets until you reach the marketplace.

Curious how clean they are, these old streets, how new and trim the houses; curious how fresh-looking the old market tower, the church of the Virgin Mary. Until suddenly you realise with a shock, all *is* brand new: stone by stone, house by house, all reconstructed on the old site, no longer Nieuport in fact but a facsimile, a duplicate. A few photographs found in any drawer will show you what existed between the ancient, unmolested Nieuport and that which stands unmolested today: a lunar landscape, a mound of ashes, a chaos of ruins, comprised of soot, fires and debris. The same experience awaits one in Dixmuiden and Langemark, a new town in place of the old, a photographic image of the old town in stone and iron, a facsimile of the past, a duplicate.

It's hard to articulate that contrary feeling when faced with such a spectacle, for one might reasonably ask, in exactly which town are you, the old or the new? Is this Nieuport or not, Dixmuiden or not? The answer is neither. It is not the new one or the old, but a doppelganger, a spectre town, who dons her old dress to haunt the daylight hours, simulating the old life but wearing new stones, just like a facsimile, unmistakable but false. And though these small towns are basking in the sun, brighter than ever, perky and fresh, though their inhabitants go leisurely about their business and their pipes leave smoke curls of contentment, you can't escape the confounding dread of the incubus, faced as one is with these Golem towns, their hasty imitation, which you cannot avoid and from which you flee as if before ghosts.

The Town without a Heart

On then, to Ypres. To left and right, the undulating gold of
ripening corn, the heaviness of the grain: one realises once more
that in nature all that is alive lives off the dead. Forests contam-
inated, their leafage yellowed by gas and eaten away, stretch
their stumps towards you as if pleading for assistance. At the
sight of numerous cemeteries here and there along the road, one
can no longer be mistaken: the theatre of a combat that lasted
four years draws near. Crosses, crosses and still more crosses,
stone armies of crosses, overwhelming spectacle when one thinks
that beneath each of these blank polished stones entwined by
roses lies a man; and without this madness, that man would be
forty or fifty today, full-blooded and in rude health. If it weren't
for such thoughts, one would be tempted to describe them as
beautiful, these death groves, harmoniously arranged in the bare
countryside, where rest Australians, Canadians, English, Bel-
gians, French and a good number of Germans too. These last
are clearly isolated from their old hostile foe – (what meaning
'hostility' for the dead?) – but hardly in the most successful way.
In fact, how moving to see them nestling together in the copses,
their wooden crosses still bright and upright even today, but
the harmonious feeling darkens into displeasure when one notes
that, unlike the English, French and Belgian cemeteries, where
officers and soldiers are obviously interred side by side, in the
German ones there exists a clinical separation, with cemeteries
for other ranks kept strictly divided. It wasn't enough that they
had different clothing, had to eat different food, travel in different train compartments, use different brothels and lavatories;
no, on top of that, having faced the same death, German army
rules sought to eternalise the appalling partition between castes,
between officer and ordinary soldier, and with these cemeteries of
first and second class is cast the shadow of what one hopes is the

death memorial of a certain military class-ethos left behind on foreign soil.

A few more narrow streets and one emerges into the market square. All seems as it once was, perfectly restored, perhaps a bit too smartly, but – horror of horrors! – the colossal cloth hall has disappeared, that cyclopean edifice, pride of Belgium, around which the entire town of little houses huddled like chicks around a mother hen. The place where this splendour heroically laboured, defying the centuries, is now only a void: like a few rotten teeth, stumps of smoke-blackened stone are turned towards the sky. The town's heart has been ripped out. Imagine if you will, to give comparison, a Berlin where the castles and the Linden²⁷ were reduced to nothing but a smoking heap of debris.

Macabre vision. More macabre than the aerial photographs in the windows that show Ypres in 1918: a landscape of craters, a vast jumble of rubble. But it was deliberate, this macabre effect, in order to retain a sense of uneasiness that this so majestic edifice was never to rise from the ashes. For it was decided that this unique building, the largest in Belgium at the outbreak of war, should remain for all time a pile of rubble, like the ruin at Heidelberg, so that generation after generation might remember. It was presumably in a spirit of vengeance that they chose to show for posterity the martyr of this town, while also looking to perpetuate the disgust and resentment felt towards the invaders. Now, if this was the initial intention, the opposite effect is produced. What was meant as a monument of war has become a monument against war. This masterpiece shattered beneath shells, virtually reduced to dust, reveals itself to be the most horrific exhortation imaginable, beseeching all those who love their country never again to expose the most sacred works of their history to such murderous destruction.

The Menin Gate

Ypres has thus been deprived of her most illustrious work of art. No one now goes, as once they might, to this withdrawn town, solely to contemplate the beautiful rectangle of those splendid halls with lines so powerful and harmonious. But in place of the lost monument, Ypres has earned a new one – a work that, allow me to say, is at first sight grandiose on an emotional level as much as an artistic one: the Menin Gate, erected by the English nation in memory of its dead, a monument so moving, which is without rival on European soil.

This colossal arch, of considerable height and clad in clear marble, ascends above the same roadway that once led to the enemy. Its shadow covers a few metres' stretch of road, the only one still open in a town surrounded, from where, under the beating sun or pouring rain, the English regiments set out for the front, where guns, ambulances, munitions were amassed and innumerable coffins were ferried to the rear. In the Roman sobriety of its proportions, mausoleum rather than Arc de Triomphe, the arch forms a broad vault. On the façade, facing the enemy, reposing on the summit, a lion in marble seems to smother beneath his claws a prey that he has no intention of setting free. On the rear section, facing the town, oppressive, sombre, stands a marble sarcophagus. This monument is dedicated to the dead, to the fifty-six thousand British soldiers who perished near Ypres and whose final resting place could not be found, those who rotted somewhere in a common grave, shredded beyond recognition by shells, or who putrefied by immersion in water; all those who lacked, unlike those in the cemeteries that ring the town, a tombstone of their own, clear, white, polished – a tangible sign of their final resting place. It is for all of them, for the fifty-six thousand soldiers, that they raised this arch of marble, this collective mausoleum, and furthermore engraved those fifty-six thousand names with gold into the marble stone; and in such profusion the letters seem, like those on the columns of the Alhambra, to have become a truly decorative pattern. A monument dedicated then not to victory but to the dead, to the victims, without the least distinction, to the Australians, to the English, to the Hindus and the Muslims, whose memory is perpetuated to an equal extent, with letters of identical size, in the same stone, so all are united in the same death. No portrait of the king, no mention of victory, no homage to the great generals, no rhetorical commentary from hereditary princes or archdukes; nothing but that inscription of such sublime brevity on the façade: '*Pro rege pro patria*.'[28] So Roman in its austereness, this tomb of fifty-six thousand men is more overwhelming than all the Arcs de Triomphe and commemorative monuments to victory that I have ever seen, and the sense of awe increases when one is privy to the scene of the stacking of wreaths, endlessly laid there by widows, children and friends. For it's an entire nation that each year gathers at this collective tomb of lost soldiers who possess no grave of their own.

Jamboree upon the Dead

Ypres has today become a site of pilgrimage for the English nation. You can understand this when you have seen the thousands upon thousands of graves, when you have encountered that tragic arch with its fifty-six thousand names. But a coming and going of such intensity constitutes a serious threat to the respect such environs inspire, and in the midst of the emotion felt, one experiences a sense of revolt against an organisation far too perfect, too precise. The marketplace is choked with automobiles, all together side by side as if before an opera, green, red, yellow coaches; hour by hour these wandering reservoirs pour their contents into the town, thousands of people, tourist armies who browse through the 'sights' (two hundred thousand graves!), accompanied by their loudly declaiming guides. For ten marks you have it all: the entire four years of war, the graves, the huge guns, the shelled cloth-hall, with lunch or dinner, all comforts and *a nice strong tea*, conforming to the information displayed on every placard. Not a shop exists where they don't profit from the dead. They even offer curios made from shell splinters (perhaps these very same shells tore out the entrails of a human being), charming souvenirs of the battlefield; the most nauseating example, I spotted in a shop window: a bronze figure of Christ whose cross was made from recovered cartridges. In the hotels music plays, the cafés are packed, automobiles crisscross the streets at a lively pace and you hear the chatter of the Kodaks. All is organised down to the last detail: twelve minutes reserved for each curiosity, for one must get back, by seven at the latest, to Blankenberge or Ostend to ensure there is time to don one's evening dress for dinner.

A horrifying fact to reflect on, throttling one almost as forcefully as the thought of the dead, that like the ground receiving its manure from corpses, the living too prosper by the dead, and the carefree descendants can observe the shocking agony of a half-million of their countrymen so comfortably and in such a well-organised fashion that they might as well be at the cinema. They roar along in cars, with good suspension, down the same roads that others travelled for months on foot, unwashed, drenched in sweat, loaded down like brick-carrying Roman slaves. They are served promptly in the well-ventilated restaurant dining rooms anything they may request to eat and drink, which for the others in their grimy fetid basements would have had the taste of nectar or ambrosia. They can, for on average ten marks, ponder at their ease, placidly, a cigarette to their lips, for a half hour or so, four years of martyrdom by half a million men, then conclude with a few dozen postcards that laud the experience as a sight worth seeing.

Nevertheless.

Nevertheless: it is good that, in some places on this earth, one can still encounter a few horrifying visible traces of the great crime. Ultimately it is something good too when a hundred thousand people, comfortable and carefree, clatter through here annually, and whether they care for it or not, these countless graves, these poisoned woods, these devastated squares still serve as reminders. And all remembering for the most primitive, the most blasé natures, is somehow visual. All that recalls the past in whatever form or intention leads the memory back towards those terrible years that must never be unlearned. In the same way, I find it right and pedagogical that each year in Belgium on 4th August at nine o'clock in the morning, at the moment when in 1914 the Germans invaded the country, all the bells begin to ring, the sirens of the factories sound and all work ceases for a few minutes. The authorities who took this decision did this with a patriotic intention to celebrate the nation, not as a sign of opposing war; nevertheless, even this measure encourages recollection, it shakes and stirs up torpid and muddied consciences. And it would be cause for celebration if all the European countries that formerly participated in the war adopted this solemn custom, so that each year, in Germany and in France too, at the precise hour when war was declared the bells began to ring, the sirens to howl, and all labour ceased for a few minutes – for five minutes of recollection, realisation and indignation.

– 1928

Salzburg – the Framed Town

The beauty of a town never rests on its architecture alone; it comes about from a particular fusion with nature, a successful marriage between the work of man and the hand of God, what has been created from human spirit and what is created in nature. To respond to this form of beauty it is not enough for a town to unite with a particular element, it must be in union with all: water, air and earth. Water confers on it a more vital aspect: in the case of a river, it divides the town and carries to it waves and ships. When it's a seaport, it carries the aroma of the far distances and the image of eternal voyage. The earth narrows in a spectacular variety of hills, mountains, rock faces, escarpments, providing a backdrop for the architecture and a vantage point for an overall view. A town situated in a plain, without water or mountains, can never really pretend to beauty. In the end, to be beautiful, a town needs air to breathe – broad squares, attractive perspectives that allow its forms to reveal themselves in their fullness.

Salzburg offers a perfect example of these three elements: earth, water, air. Approaching from the south the most powerful massif of rock in Europe, the Alps, advances menacingly, but just before Salzburg, or to be precise in the very town itself, the wave of rock suddenly ceases to rear up and gives way altogether. The Untersberg, the Watzmann, the Göll, high mountains of two thousand metres, rise above the valley like a wall and ring the horizon. Yet they do not fall in a brutal way into the depths, but rather evolve into a series of modest gentle hills of which a pair, the Mönchsberg and the Kapuzinerberg, are found within the borders of the town itself, in a fabric of greenery, domesticated, inhabited; and after these last herd-like forms, the flat land begins, which like the palm of a hand rises towards the North Sea. On the right one's gaze is lifted to the snow-capped summits and rocky escarpments, while on the left it embraces a panorama that is clear to infinity. So then, this town is situated exactly at the boundary between two vital spaces, between two kinds of climate, between mountain landscape and the lowland plain. It can be both wholly a city of the north and a city of the south, with its heights muffled in white, its air limpid, glacial, where you hear the sound of sleighs crossing the pristine expanses and skiers swooping down the hills and mountains. But from one day to the next the wind changes; with the effect of the föhn the sky becomes bluer, humid and warm, then suddenly Salzburg becomes a town of the south, with the colours of Italy shining out with its white houses, its garlands of blooming gardens; in such moments a final beam of brightness from the south lightly touches this so deeply Germanic town.

Water, the second component of beauty, is equally linked to Salzburg. A Nordic poet, Jens Peter Jacobsen, made the river Salzach, which crosses with its often rapid and turbulent waves, the fulcrum of one of his most enchanting short stories. It's an alpine river, small but rebellious, which in a mean mood can boil up during the melting period, impetuously crashing into the bridges and dragging along with it, by way of plunder, innumerable trees; in summer it seems on the whole to be calm, tranquil, but will rarely accept to bear any more than a canoe on its restless back. However, this is not the only aquatic component to bring life to this landscape; all around, to the depths of the Salzkammergut and in the direction of Berchtesgaden, lie a series of lakes, on open ground, overshadowed or encircled by mountains, green or blue, large or small, plain or romantic; you could say that comely nature has scattered in the verdure an infinite number of mirrors in which to muse on its charms, each time in a different way. Third component of beauty: air, free space. Prodigality presided over the construction of Salzburg:

imposing towers, mighty palaces, churches of insolent dimensions, and before all these edifices spacious squares, emphas-
ising their size and shape to perfection. Twenty, thirty church
towers rise from this ancient Episcopal seat, slender and round-
domed, square and ending in a bulb shape, small and so discreet
they seem like hats pointing above the houses; while others,
broader, immense, deliberately seek to echo St Peter's in Rome
and all its splendour. Each of these churches has bells and all
of them chime, each with a different tone, more or less clear and
in such a way that at certain hours the town seems overhung
by a vault of bronze. Dominating the ensemble stands with all
its weight the emblem of the town, the Hohensalzburg fortress,
offering a dramatic and always changing perspective.[29] One
can descend the Gaisberg to the valley or come by way of the
Bavarian plain, so one's gaze can plunge from the heights or rise
towards them – on all sides, from north, south, west and east,
from near and far, the first thing one sees is that unmistakable
eyrie formed of stone, the Hohensalzburg, above the undula-
tions of the landscape. Anchored there since Roman times, a
2,000-year-old trireme of bright stone, this ship crosses time,
resting in the same place for all eternity; now it offers the blinding vision of its bow with mast and pennant, now it turns
towards you its flanks with their hundreds of hatches and windows. And the ancient little town rustles around the brilliant
ship like wash amidst a green tide.

The town is very ancient; offering the same outline over centuries, it has changed little, and today they keep a watchful eye
to preserve it as intact as possible, that extraordinary historical
picture of a medieval city at the heart of modern life. By happy
chance, it was the only one, in a German empire so endlessly
restless with bellicose spirit, not to have known war for many
centuries, not to have been conquered or destroyed, and so

what was created over such a long period by our ancestors could be faithfully preserved in its original form. The wealth of Salzburg, as its name suggests, comes from salt. For in those European countries far from the coast, which could not receive that manna from the sea, salt was as precious as gold, and from all the places in Europe where it could be found paths were sewn, those quite unique roads, the salt routes. They used them to transport by boat or cart the priceless substance, so indispensable to food. The fact that salt was extracted close to Salzburg at Hallein, at Hallstatt – 'hall' always signifies salt – was known by the Romans, who with their remarkable feel for strategy quickly understood the exceptional character of Salzburg's geographical situation, making it their Fort Juvavum. Still, even today, with almost every demolition they discover stones or fragments of Roman vases. Then the town passed into the hands of the archbishops who despised war and were enthusiasts of art. The construction of sumptuous churches, vast palaces, beautiful gardens, fountains and water games, such were their passions; they invited Italian architects and musicians, and used their fortunes to make the city magnificent. Also, thanks to the wisdom of their politics, which meant Salzburg was sheltered from all war, their work remained unchanged, and so when one walks, particularly in the evening, through streets or across squares, the illusion is complete; one might think oneself truly in the fifteenth or sixteenth century, for at the heart of the town proper there is virtually no building dating from less than three hundred years ago, and where renovations have proved necessary, they are carried out with the precaution of retaining the style of the past.

All this makes Salzburg a city of two faces, mysterious and difficult to compare to any other. It is very ancient, old fashioned, and yet in summer it can be the liveliest, most culturally vibrant town in all Europe. The festival sees the great cavalcades of luxury bringing here vast fortunes, the most famous personalities, the most questing spirits of Europe, and for two months Salzburg is the European capital of music, theatre and literature par excellence. One is fully immersed in the twentieth century, and then some fifty paces further on one finds oneself in a tranquil churchyard, unchanged for half a millennium, old courtyards with old tools, still slumbering in the middle ages. Barely realising, one leaves nature behind and is in the town, then one leaves the town and is again in nature. In meadows surrounding an old castle avenues appear that suddenly become roads, their trees freeze, transform into blocks of stone. On the other side, inside the town, spacious gardens blossom into courtyards, unknown to all; villas and modest palaces assure the transition between the high and the low, between mountain, hill and valley. Nowhere does one find sharp rupture; nature penetrates softly into the town, which in return opens its fan across the countryside. The old integrates with the new, modernity with the obsolete, north with south; mountain and valley are here reconciled.

This art of harmonious transition gives the town a wonderful character and, at the same time, an eminently musical air. Like other towns, Salzburg manages to resolve melodiously in stone and through atmosphere that which is usually crudely opposed in reality. This secret, this resolution of dissonances, the town has been taught by music. Is it really necessary to remember – if you needed further proof of its musicality – that here is found the birthplace of Mozart. That the most gifted, the most spirited, the most supple, the most passionate of all musicians was born here cannot be chance. Having encountered at the heart of the landscape a grandeur and a formal rigour, and in the charming gardens, in the ornate baroque of Episcopal buildings, that melody inherent to the town's architecture, he raised them to another domain, to eternal harmony. How, exactly, such a town creates itself is as hard to explain as the creation of a work of art – and it matters little to ask who wanted for it that powerful musical shading, still audible even to the deafest ear, that the town is known for. Perhaps it can be attributed to the archbishops, those illuminated rich amateurs of art, to the magic of the landscape, to Italian architects, or to the unique constellation of the epoch. A spell always guards something unexplained. Just as above certain people, the genius of music glides above certain places, making their very envelope of stone resonate in a particular way. Unlike most German cities crammed inside a belt of walls, Salzburg had the good fortune not to be constructed with a view to defence and war. Its soul has at all times been able to express itself, to sing and vibrate, a resounding instrument at the service of a celebration of moments both solemn and joyful. They built squares for processions; palaces for pleasure, games and gaiety; churches with vaults destined for the organ and the hymn – from the very beginning the masters of this town, attracted by art and pomp, had deliberately instilled a festive, playful atmosphere, and one of its citizens – Mozart, the eternal son – elevated it from stone and line into spirit and music. Through him the form of the town, in this other sphere, has achieved eternity – today the forsaken instrument sounds again, in this natural frame, so perfect for a festival and for joyfulness. In Salzburg there is no need, as in a theatre, to erect a false background of canvas and cardboard to create an ambiance and give theatrical illusion. For *Jedermann* or for *Faust* for example, lane, courtyard, church and landscape already constitute a decor without rival and contribute to creating an atmosphere. The greatest, the finest artists of our time feel lighter here than in their frames of planks smelling of dust and mould; the singers' voices rise more clearly, more fully; and during the festival all accords in a climate of true festivity. But that is hardly surprising, for when the first notes ring out, when the festival begins, it is not something from outside, but something new that is grafted forcefully onto the town's atmosphere: the will of its masters from the past, engraved in the stone, music frozen there in the walls, which resounds and holds you in its spell. And on those rare days when one sees the union of sky and landscape and the most eminent artists of the time in the most sublime works, such as *Fidelio*, *The Magic Flute* or *Orpheus and Eurydice*, at the heart of a shattered world, in these shattered times, one feels sometimes borne towards the solemn spheres, one experiences that state of grace uniquely produced when nature and art, art and nature exchange a kiss, and on such days, this thousand-year-old town accomplishes its mission not only for its country, but for the entire world.

– 1935

The House of a Thousand Fortunes
(Written for the fiftieth anniversary of the 'Shelter' in London)

These days, journeying from one country to another, by train or ship, if you have the time that is and possess the gift of observation, you will continually be struck by the number of travellers whose conduct abruptly changes as they approach the frontier. They become restless, unable to remain in one place; they come and go with a noticeable air of tension about them. An anxiety has taken hold, that's plain to see, a quite mysterious anxiety. Indeed, within the hour, or half hour, a foreign land will emerge, and with it great uncertainty. One is detached from all normality; customs are different, as are laws and language, so the agitation that awaits the newcomer has already taken possession of their entire being. Their worries are actually physically perceptible, as with jittery fingers they obsessively pat the inside pocket that holds their passport, papers and the little money they possess. In their home country, they were assured all was in order; they had paid their stamps and fees. But, but... will any of that be worth a thing? What if the door of this new country slams shut in their faces at the last moment? They pace up and down, their vexation grows, suddenly the frontier is nearing. And when, seized with pity, you look at them, they return that look with such timidity. You sense it, they want to question you, converse with you, be reassured, consoled in their apprehension, secure a friend, some support in this foreign country that now opens up before them. But at the same time they are suspicious: back home they have been warned about assaults by strangers who wish to deprive them of even the most miserable of their few paltry belongings. So they duck their heads once more, wary and frightened, until the moment arrives when they present themselves before the customs official like the accused before his judge.

Today, thousands upon thousands of such people are on the move and amongst them many are Jews. Once again a terrific hurricane has broken on the world, tearing from the millennial tree its leaves and sending them swirling along the highways of the earth. Yet again, like their fathers and ancestors, a numberless mass of Jews are forced to leave their country, a home where they existed in peace, and find themselves, without most of the time knowing where, another homeland. But in no epoch has the struggle to find sanctuary in a foreign country been as arduous as in the present day, as countries isolate themselves behind hostility and jealousy. Mistrust among men has never been so refined and he who is today a stateless person is disadvantaged as never before.

Observe them well, then, these stateless persons, you who have the good luck to know your house and country, you who on return from some journey find your room and bed all prepared, you who have the books you cherish around you, the tools to which you are accustomed. Observe them well, these rootless ones, you who have the good luck to know what you are living from and for whom, in order better to understand and with humility to see how chance has favoured you above these others. Observe them well, these men crammed into the stern of a boat, and go to them, speak to them, for even this simple approach of drawing a little nearer is for them some consolation; and while you address them in their language they may unconsciously inhale a whiff of the air of their native land, their eyes will light up and become eloquent. Ask them where they are heading! The faces darken. To South America, they reply, the relatives are there. But on what will they live when they arrive, will they find work and construct a new life for themselves? Then you ask them how long they will stay in London. Oh, only three days, until the next boat. Do they speak the language? No. Do they know anyone there who might help them?

No. Do they have sufficient funds to find lodgings? No. How then are they going to come through these three days and nights? Then, assured and confident, they smile, 'That's all in hand. We are staying at the shelter.'

The shelter? I had never heard of it, despite residing in London for some time. Never has anyone alerted me to this place, this institution. But the curious thing is that all these Jews coming from the most distant and exotic destinations are fully aware of its existence. In Poland, the Ukraine, Latvia and Bulgaria, from one end of Europe to the other, all the poor Jews know the London shelter. Like the same star seen by numberless people who know nothing of each other, its name represents for them a kind of communion in reassurance. Right across the Jewish world it spreads by word of mouth, the legend of the London shelter: somewhere there is a place where the wandering Jew (and how many are obliged now to be so!) can find rest for a weary body and solace for the soul, a place that grants them a few precious days of calm and helps them to continue on their way from one foreign country to another. And the fact that I and precisely I alone, who had so often stayed in London, appeared to be the only Jew on that boat who had never heard of the place, filled me with shame. Such is the nature of things: of all the ills that occur in the world we are informed. Each morning the paper barks in your face wars, murders and crimes, the madness of politics clutters our senses, but the good that happens quietly unnoticed, of that we are scarcely aware. Such things are all the more crucial in an epoch like ours, for all ethical labour by its example wakens in us truly precious energies, and each man becomes the better when he is capable of admiring with sincerity that which is inherently good.

With that in mind, I went to visit this shelter. It's a house in the East End, an unremarkable street and yet all distresses have somehow found their way there. Decorated in a functional manner, eschewing luxury but scrupulously clean, doors ever-wide-open await the traveller, the emigrant wishing to make his halt there. There is a bed at his disposal and a laid table and, moreover, he can receive advice and assistance in the heart of a foreign world. The anxiety that tormented him, he can finally express without concern before friendly people, ready to help him; they will think, they will write for him and they will look to smooth out a part of the unknown and painful road stretching before him. Adrift in the terrifying insecurity that has enveloped the lives of thousands like a glacial mist, at least for a few days he may feel the warmth and light of humanity – truly consoled at the heart of all this hopelessness he sees, he experiences it: that he is not alone and abandoned in this foreign country, no, rather he is linked to a community of his people and to the still higher community of mankind in general.

Naturally a lengthy stay is not granted to any one of them, for the destitution of the Jewish people today crosses the world like a ceaseless river. Another expelled person will find rest to-morrow in this bed; another will eat at that table: for fifty years, since its foundation, thousands upon thousands have found rest and recovered their strength in this shelter and have left it filled with gratitude. No poet would possess the imagination to paint the diversity and tragedy of these thousands of fates. Indeed, wherever fresh despair washes over the world, whether in Germany, Poland or Spain, it carries with it these shattered existences, these crumbs – ignored by the contented, the wealthy, the freewheeling – to that house, which until now spectacularly resisted every onslaught and whose custodians completed their labour of assistance with a dedication worthy of our profound admiration. Even if they could only draw one drop from the relentless tide of human misery, the Jewish misery, what a significant achievement that would already represent, to accord a single day of joy to some unfortunate, to grant a stateless person, if only for a few hours' grace, the feeling that he is home, to give a fresh sense of assurance to a truly desperate being! That's why the work of this house that helps the homeless and exiled is so admirable! Let us thank all those who created and maintain it, this peerless yet unknown monument to mankind's solidarity!

– 1937

Gardens in Wartime

Along with so many in Europe, I have now had the sad privilege of sharing, with unconditional clarity, a second World War, and in so doing I will have seen each of these wars from a different front. The first I saw from Germany and Austria, the second from England. That is why my observations lead me, in spite of myself, constantly to propose comparisons that have a bearing not only on the configuration of both wars, but also on both warring peoples.

From the very first day I sensed a marked difference. In 1914 the declaration of war in Vienna meant a kind of ecstasy, a state of drunkenness. People had only known about war through books, they had not thought it possible such a thing could happen again in these civilised times. Now, suddenly, there it was, and since no one had any idea just how horrible, how murderous it would be, the imagination suddenly aroused in these men brimming with infantile curiosity was inflamed, transforming war into a romantic adventure. Vast hordes streamed from houses and businesses into the streets to form enthusiastic columns; suddenly flags appeared, no one knew where from; there was music, people sang in chorus, cheered and shouted with joy, no one knew why. The young men massed before the offices to enlist. They had only one fear: to be called up too late and miss the great adventure. And above all, each felt the need to speak, to speak of what created a communal state of excitation. Strangers came together in the street; in the offices they forgot about office work, in the shops about sales; people simply telephoned each other incessantly house by house, to ease their inner tension through words; the restaurants and Viennese coffee houses were packed for weeks on end late into the night with people bent on discussion, exultant, nervous types who chattered on and on, each one a strategist, an economist, a prophet.

Such is the unforgettable image that stays with me from the Vienna of 1914. And then England, 1939: a contrast no less unforgettable. In 1939 war did not arise suddenly, it simply gave concrete form to fears already present. Since Hitler's seizure of power, in every country they had seen it coming, closer and closer, doing all they could to keep it at bay, knowing the horror it signified. They knew from their own experience, from observation, that this was no romantic mythical creature, but a gigantic machine, equipped with every conceivable fiendish art of technology, whose daily revolution demanded a colossal quantity of men and money in order to function. People were under no illusions. No one cheered, each was scared, each was conscious that his country, that the world stood on the brink of a dark epoch. They endured the war because it was necessary to do so, as something inevitable.

That was in 1939, yet although I knew that – and yes, I expected a certain natural stoicism – England had surprises in store, and during these days of war I learnt more about this people than I had in all the previous years. It started from the very first day. I had need of an administrative document, and the official was in the process of providing it when the door opened. Another official entered and announced 'Germany has invaded Poland. It's war. *I have to leave at once.*' He pronounced these words in a perfectly calm voice, as if he were transmitting a minor bureaucratic communication. And while my heart skipped a beat and I (why was I so ashamed?) felt my finger trembling, the unruffled official before me completed his document and handed it to me with that light amicable smile of the English. Had he not understood? Did he not believe the news? But I stepped out into the street. All was peaceful, the people were not walking at a quickened pace or in an excited manner. They are not aware yet, I still thought. Otherwise they would not go about their business so equably, with such impassivity in their respective occupations.

But now came the flickering white of the newspapers, blowing about. People bought them, read them and continued on their way. No high-spirited groups, even in the shops no anxious gatherings. And so it was week after week, each fulfilling his function placidly, without agitation, silently and replete with calm resolve: had there not been certain visible signs like the *black-out* or the unusually high frequency of uniforms, none would infer, from the comportment of the people alone, that this country was fighting one of the most exacting and crucial wars of its history.

Such composure, then, in these moments when all other countries can barely suppress their disquietude, their excitation, their passion, presents us, we who are not English, with the mysterious nature of the English character. So often has one tried to provide a psychological explanation for this self-mastery: an innate tightening of the nerves; the educational system, which from childhood teaches them to conceal feelings, or at least not to display them publicly. But we underestimate, I believe, a deeper element: the constant union with nature that transmits unseen a measure of its composure to each individual in a perpetual union, one on one. I have long believed – like most – that the English love nothing more than their house. But in truth what they really love is their garden. A recent census shows there are three and a half million of these – virtually every house has one, even the smallest, and a large number of Londoners living in flats possess a second home, a weekend retreat whose garden and flowers they yearn for all week long. Thus millions of English people, the allegedly so unromantic English, are, at weekends or after work, found labouring in their garden or allotment: evenings or mornings, the worker, the clerk, the minister, the businessman, the priest reach for their tools, put spade to earth, prune the shrubs or take care of their flowers. In this *gardening*, this daily activity that is not sport, nor work, nor a game, but where all those activities gradually coalesce, the English earn their solidarity, social differences disappear, the distance between rich and poor is abolished: the earls or dukes themselves, with a dozen or so gardeners in their service, are no less personally attached to their garden than the mechanic with a few miserable square feet of greenery at the rear of his house. And a half-hour or hour spent daily in the company of flowers, of trees, of fruits, in the company of the eternal in nature, that hour or half-hour during which they are totally detached from events and matters on the outside seems to me, by its power of *relaxing*, to be at the origin of this marvellous calm the English people enjoy, which to us remains incomprehensible, or at least inaccessible. At the heart of a world so unstable and on the brink of destruction, they are reminded each day of what constitutes the essential on our earth: that its beauty protects from the insanity of wars and the absurdity of politics. At the beginning of a new day or at its end, they have acquired, thanks to this communion with nature, a fortitude and sense of calm that, on a scale of several million individuals, determines a trait of the national character. These countless modest little gardens, pressed up against the most shabby houses, with their handful of shrubs, their crown of flowers, their square of allotment – it is these that exercise such a considerable palliative effect on the people, insulating them from nervous excitement, from uncertainty and the drone of chatter. Thanks to them, the individual may renew each day his calm and sangfroid – barely conceivable for us who are not English – giving the entire nation its strength; and in so doing offering us the grand spectacle of moral constancy, a spectacle almost as great as that of nature itself.

– 1940

The Langerei, Bruges

Palace of the Popes, Avignon

The Alyscamps, Arles

Grote Markt, Antwerp

Tyne Cot military cemetery, Passchendaele, near Ypres

Salzburg from the Kapuzinerberg

Notes

1. Vineta: a town, possibly legendary, often claimed to have been located on the Polish island of Wolin in the Baltic Sea.
2. 'Instead of the great vessels that moved about on them.' Zweig is referring to a line in a poem from the collection *Le Règne du Silence* (1891) by Georges Rodenbach. It is interesting to note that Zweig's rendering of the line, presumably from memory, was incorrect in terms of both grammar and content. The actual line Rodenbach used in his poem was '*Au lieu des vaisseaux vains, qui s'agitaient en elles,*' meaning literally, 'Instead of the futile vessels that moved about on them.'
3. Zweig refers to the celebrated portrait of Georges Rodenbach by Lévy-Dhurmer, then in the musée du Luxembourg, now in the musée d'Orsay, Paris.
4. A museum in Avignon.
5. An area of heath-land in north-eastern Germany.
6. Zweig refers to the legend of Tristan and Isolde.
7. Name taken from Norse or north German mythology. Also refers to Wagner's Ring cycle.
8. Chinese shadows.
9. Two sea monsters of Greek legend said to be situated on either side of the straits of Messina between Calabria and Sicily in Italy.
10. Zweig refers to Schiller's 'The Siege of Antwerp'.
11. The 'Hanse' or 'Hanseatic league' was an alliance of trading cities and guilds that stretched along the northern European coast.
12. Zweig refers to Christophe Plantin, master printer of Antwerp, born around the year 1520.
13. A Flemish Renaissance architect and sculptor (1514–75) who played a vital role in Antwerp's construction.
14. Jan Steen and Gerhard Terborch were seventeenth-century Dutch genre painters.
15. Zweig refers to Tomas de Torquemada, murderous leader of the Spanish Inquisition.
16. Historical residence of the king of Spain.
17. 'A young Andalusian woman will look with impassioned eyes at a passing cart, a dog that chases its own tail.'
18. An Alpine wind that occurs in the lee of a mountain range.
19. The second longest river in Spain after the Tagus.
20. 'Whoever has not seen Seville, has not seen a marvel.'
21. A trick-taking card game for three players once very popular in nineteenth century Germany.
22. Legendary king who invented the art of brewing beer.
23. Boulevard Saint-Michel.
24. French poet, dramatist and diplomat (1868–1955), the younger brother of the sculptor Camille Claudel.

25. In the book of my memory.

26. *The Mastersingers* is an opera in three acts by Richard Wagner.

27. Zweig refers to the lime trees, *Den Linden*, that famously lined the avenue Unter den Linden in Berlin.

28. 'For my king, for my country.'

29. Hohensalzburg: this ancient fortress stands atop a sheer rock wall that hems in on one side the ancient centre of Salzburg. It entirely dominates the town. Zweig's image of a ship is apt, since the fortification is broadside on to the town 'showing its flanks', with its prow-like southernmost end driving through the rock and clinging vegetation of the Mönchsberg.

List of essays

Ypren, 1928
(Ypres)

Salzburg – die Stadt als Rahmen, 1933
(Salzburg – The Framed Town)

Das Haus der tausend Schicksale, 1937
(House of A Thousand Fates)

Die Gärten im Kriege, 1940
(Gardens in Wartime)

Biographical note

Stefan Zweig was born in Vienna on 28th November 1881, to a respected, wealthy family who ensured he was given the best education in both academic and cultural terms. Zweig quickly found his way into the intellectual and artistic circles of the Hapsburg capital. He studied philosophy, joined literary groups and then started writing poetry, which was soon published. Financially secure, Zweig went on to travel widely, form important contacts in literature and the arts across Europe and become an extremely prolific writer. He wrote dramas, short stories and novels and made translations of French poetry into German. As well as countless reviews, articles and introductions to books, he also wrote biographies and monographs on writers and historical figures who fascinated him and with whom he often felt a particular kinship. These and a series of arresting and psychologically penetrating novellas and short stories earned him worldwide fame by the thirties. A staunch pacifist, Zweig dreamt of a united Europe where nationalism was eradicated and cultural progress could flourish without borders. The First World War dealt a near fatal blow to this dream, which finally collapsed with the rise of Nazism and the second instalment of world war. Following a police raid on his Salzburg home, Zweig left Austria in 1934 and found sanctuary in England while in Germany his books burned. No longer able to publish in Germany, Zweig was definitively exiled and when war reached England in 1939, the Jewish pacifist writer was deemed an enemy alien due to his native sovereignty. He travelled to the USA and then decided to shelter in Brazil until the war ended. But prone to depression and cut off from his beloved Europe, which appeared to have destroyed itself, and increasingly pessimistic about the future, he committed suicide with his wife Lotte Altmann in their house near Petropolis on 22nd February 1942.

Will Stone, born in 1966, is a poet who divides his time between the UK and Belgium. In November 2008 his first collection of poems, *Glaciation*, won the coveted international Glen Dimplex Award for poetry. His published translations include *To the Silenced* (selected poems of Georg Trakl, 2005) and the sonnet sequence *Les Chimères* by Gérard de Nerval (1999). His translations also appeared in the Tate anthology of German Expressionist Poetry (2003). In 2010 he will also publish two collections of poetry by Francophone Belgian poets Emile Verhaeren and Georges Rodenbach in a first modern English translation. Will has contributed reviews, essays, poems and translations to a number of leading journals and literary papers in the UK and abroad, including *The Times Literary Supplement*, *The London Magazine*, *Irish Pages* and *The Guardian* and *Independent* newspapers. His future projects include a second collection of poetry in 2011, a translation of Maeterlinck's influential first collection of poems *Serres Chauds* (1889) and a collection of essays relating to Belgium.

Acknowledgements

I would like to express my gratitude to the following who in their individual capacities, have contributed to the publication and promotion of this book. Without their generous advice, expertise and enthusiasm, this collection would not be in the hands of English readers today. Sincere thanks go to Sonja Dobbins, Dr Martin Liebscher, Professor Rudiger Göerner, and especially Marie-Pierre Devroedt in Brussels. I should also like to thank the Stefan Zweig Centre in Salzburg and the Austrian Cultural Institute in London for their interest and support.

– *Will Stone*

HESPERUS PRESS

Hesperus Press is committed to bringing near what is far –
far both in space and time. Works written by the greatest
authors, and unjustly neglected or simply little known in the
English-speaking world, are made accessible through new
translations and a completely fresh editorial approach. Through
these classic works, the reader is introduced to the greatest
writers from all times and all cultures.

For more information on Hesperus Press, please visit our website:
www.hesperuspress.com

  MODERN VOICES